DEBATING MODERATE ISLAM

DEBATING MODERATE ISLAM

The Geopolitics of Islam and the West

Edited by

M. A. MUQTEDAR KHAN

THE UNIVERSITY OF UTAH PRESS
Salt Lake City

The Defiance House Man colophon is a registered trademark of the University of Utah Press. It is based upon a four-foot-tall, Ancient Puebloan pictograph (late PIII) near Glen Canyon, Utah.

11 10 09 08 07   1 2 3 4 5

LIBRARY OF CONGRESS CATALOGING-IN-PUBLICATION DATA

Debating moderate Islam : the geopolitics of Islam and the West / edited by M.A. Muqtedar Khan.
     p. cm.
   Includes index.
   ISBN 978-0-87480-901-5 (pbk. : alk. paper) 1. Islam and world politics. 2. Islam—21st century. 3. Islamic renewal. 4. Religious pluralism—Islam. 5. Islamic countries—Relations—Europe. 6. Europe—Relations—Islamic countries. I. Khan, M. A. Muqtedar.
   BP173.5.D483 2007
   320.5'57—dc22

                                                    2007021527

Printed and bound by Sheridan Books, Inc., Ann Arbor, Michigan

This book is for Reshma, Rumi, and Ruhi,

my wife and children,

whose love and support provide invaluable

comfort and hope

Contents

PREFACE

THE DEBATE ON THE MODERATION of Islamic teachings and the over-whelming majority of moderate Muslims is critical to the future of peaceful relations between the United States/West and the Muslim World and its Western diasporas. So far U.S. and Western interests are being challenged by a small radical minority of Muslims who are seeking political and geopolitical transformation, first in the Muslim World and then globally. As long as groups such as al-Qaeda are recognized for what they are—a fringe minority—the mainstream Muslim community will remain an ally in the struggle against violent extremism. If we conflate radical Muslims with the rest of the Muslim World and blame extremism on Islamic values per se, however, then there is no hope for peace or peaceful relations between the Muslim World and the West.

It is of utmost importance for both the Muslim World and the West to recognize the existence and significance of moderate Islam. This book and the debate it presents are of vital strategic value and, we hope, will have an impact on policy discussions. It is with great pride that I present these wide-ranging ideas and perspectives on what constitutes moderate Islam and the role it can play in bridging the divide between Islam and the West.

This book owes a great debt to the Association of Muslim Social Scientists for giving me the opportunity to convene this important debate. I am grateful to the editorial board of the *American Journal of Islamic Social Sciences* for responding to the idea so positively and offering me the assistance and support necessary to bring it to fruition. Thanks are due to the International Institute of Islamic Thought for providing a research grant to support the project. I am also grateful to all the contributors, who so enthusiastically participated in the project.

Special thanks are due to Hakan Yavuz, for helping with the book project. As always I am grateful to my wife, Reshma, and my children, Rumi and Ruhi, for enriching my life.

M. A. MUQTEDAR KHAN
Newark, Delaware
October 23, 2006

DEBATING MODERATE ISLAM

{I}

INTRODUCTION

Chapter 1

DEBATING MODERATE ISLAM

M. A. MUQTEDAR KHAN

S INCE THE ATTACKS ON AMERICA ON SEPTEMBER 11, 2001, we have had several conversations about the different interpretations of Islam and its impact on Muslim politics and the relationship between Islam and the West. This debate has gained renewed vigor after the London attacks on July 7, 2005. Scholars and policymakers are in agreement that a politically angry and intellectually narrow interpretation of Islam—referred to loosely as militant or radical Islam—is exacerbating already rampant anti-Americanism in the Muslim World and encouraging terrorist responses to real and perceived injustices. Some analysts assert the complete innocence of the United States and blame radical Islamists alone for all the problems in the world, while others completely ignore the existence of extremism in the Muslim World and blame the United States for all the ills of our times. Most people are somewhere in between.

Regardless of where one stands in this debate, there is now growing consensus that those on the moderate side in the Muslim World must assert themselves and join the battle against extremism. Governments in the West are being advised that it is important for them to recruit the help and cooperation of moderate Muslims in order to ensure that the war against extremism does not become or appear to be a war against Islam. This policy idea of including moderate Muslims as allies against extremism in the Muslim World has generated an interesting debate about what moderation really means and who is a moderate Muslim.

From the earliest period, after the death of the Prophet of Islam (peace be upon him) Muslims have interpreted Islam in diverse ways. Many interpretations of what constitutes the Islamic Shariah—the essence of Islamic message—have been offered, some even contradictory. But Muslims have recognized difference and diversity as a consequence of divine purpose and developed a culture of tolerance for different manifestations and interpretations of Islam. From the very beginning there have been varying interpretations of Islam: Shia and Sunni, rational and traditional, mystical and philosophical, cultural and juristic. So it is more accurate to talk about Islams rather than Islam. For academic as well as strategic purposes, it is absolutely necessary to distinguish between different Islams and not to paint with a broad brush, which will inevitably lead to bad analysis and bad policy.

For the purposes of U.S. foreign policy, however, it is important to distinguish between two broad competing historical tendencies within Islamic history. One of these two tendencies can be characterized as a defensive mechanism that seeks to conserve, preserve, and defend "Islam" and eventually leads to narrow, combative, and often intolerant interpretations of Islam and who is a good Muslim. In our times we associate this tendency very strongly with Salafi and Wahhabi groups. But we must be careful to recognize that religious intolerance does not necessarily lead to political confrontation, violence, terrorism, and anti-Americanism. While al-Qaeda is definitely Salafi-Wahhabi and is a threat to the United States, the Saudi royal family and the Qataris and the Kuwaitis are also mostly Salafi-Wahhabis but are America's friends and allies.

The alternative is a more liberal and compassionate, even mystical interpretation of Islam, which is highly accommodating of difference within Islam and between religions. It is compatible with democracy and religious pluralism and is often referred to as liberal Islam or moderate Islam.

WHAT IS RADICAL ISLAM?

Since September 11 some analysts have had a strong tendency to construct the enemy as a discrete, ideological, and institutionalized actor called radical Islam or radical fundamentalist fascist Islam. Radical Islam is imagined as a manifestation of Islam that is narrow, intolerant, authoritarian, violent, anti-West, antidemocracy, anti-American, and anti-Israel. There is no doubt that a very angry and vicious tendency is growing within the Muslim World, but we must be careful not to lump all instances of Muslim conservatism and even militancy under the label of radical Islam and thereby ignore both their theological and political diversity. For example, Hizbollah and Hamas are very different from each other: the former is Shia, the later is Sunni; the former is motivated by geopolitics, and the latter is struggling for independence. Neither shares theological or political goals with al-Qaeda. For instance, Hamas has never targeted the United

States. Also consider the Wahhabis and Salafis: while al-Qaeda surely is anti-American, not all Saudis, Kuwaitis, and Qataris, who share the same theology, are anti-American or violent.

My humble suggestion is to view the various trends—political and theological—as options. Today the Muslim World has reached nearly universal consensus on three issues. First, political, social, normative, cultural, economic, and structural change must occur. Muslims are struggling to respond to the challenges of modernity and postmodernity, not to mention the global geopolitical realities of the postcolonial world. Second, most Muslims agree that no security exists in Muslim societies; they are victims of terrorism and war. Third, there is also a strong consensus that Islam must play a role in the resurgence, reconstitution, revival, development, and transformation of the Muslim World.

I submit to you that all these movements in the Muslim World (secular Bathism, Islamism, resurgent Sufism, the calls for Islamic democracy or for liberal democracy and revolution) are attempts to cope with the relative backwardness of the Muslim World, its tensions with modernity, which is driven by Western culture, and its inability to secure itself. Islamists as well as the secular and moderate elite have a vision to offer. The battle of competing visions will not be won through rhetoric and discourse; it must come through action. The vision that delivers reform, change, empowerment, and security will win. So far Islamists have done a better job than most in the Arab world, unlike South Asia and East Asia. Moderate and liberal Muslims can win the battle for the soul of Islam only if they are able to deliver. To this point they have failed. So far everyone has failed except for the radicals, who at least hit back against those that Muslims perceive as enemies.

Muslims have turned to the option of radical Islam due to the failure of all other ideas and movements to deliver a stable, prosperous, and peaceful state and society for ordinary Muslims. Radical Muslims also offer an explanation of global politics and recent history that glorifies Islam, privileges Muslim tradition, and sometimes is consistent with a simplistic view of reality. For example, the 2006 war in Lebanon goes a long way to convince Muslims that radical Islamists are right when they say that Israel is out to destroy their nations with the help of the United States.

Political, military, economic, and intellectual independence from the West has always been the overriding goal of political Islam. The failure of Islamists to achieve these goals in nearly a century, however, in combination with real and perceived injustices committed by America and its allies against Muslims, has engendered an extremely vitriolic hatred of the United States in the hearts of some Islamists, giving birth to radical Islam. I like to call these radicals *rogue Islamists,* who are willing to do absolutely anything to destroy America and its power and will to prevent the realization of Islamist goals. Rogue Islamists and their hateful discourses are globalizing anti-Americanism and in the process undermining the moral fabric of the Muslim World and corrupting Islam's message of justice, mercy, submission, compassion, and enlightenment, not of war, hatred, and killing.

Radical Islamists are a threat to both America and mainstream Islam. Their discourses are perverting Islam and generating hatred against the West, modernity, the United States, and other Muslims who disagree with them. Their most powerful weapons are their ideas and their ability to convince Muslims even to give up their lives in order to hurt America, Americans, and U.S. interests. While the United States seeks security from the attacks by rogue Muslims and needs to reduce anti-Americanism, moderate Muslims who do not subscribe to the discourse of the rogue Islamists seek to rescue Islam and innocent Muslims from their negative influence.

A response to rogue Islamists requires a complex strategy that above all must counter and delegitimize their worldview and discourse and expose their fallacies and the devastating consequences that they could bring to Muslims and the world by triggering a long and bloody global conflict between America and the Muslim World. It is my contention that the best antidote to radical Islam is liberal Islam. Liberal Islam can not only challenge the radical Islamist worldview by using Islam as the foundational idiom but also provide an alternate interpretation of Muslim reality and a more positive vision of the future.

Moderate Muslims have a very idealistic view of the Islamic duty of *jihad.* They argue, based on a tradition of the Prophet Muhammad (peace be upon him), that jihad is essentially a struggle to purify the self and to establish social justice. The highest form of jihad, *jihad-e-akbar* (the superior jihad), is struggle against the self to improve and excel in the moral and spiritual realm. The lowest form of jihad is the military jihad that is essentially defensive and constrained by strict ethics of engagement. They correctly point out that terrorism or *hirabah* (war against society) is strictly forbidden by Islamic scholars. They do maintain, however, that Muslims can and must struggle for justice and freedom while strictly obeying Islamic and international norms of just warfare. For Muslim moderates, Islam is a religion of peace without being pacifist.

Moderate Muslims are critical of U.S. foreign policy in the Muslim World. They are also critical of the prejudiced view of Islam in the West and in particular among the policy elite, who are themselves quite ignorant about Islam and the Muslim World. But Muslim moderates do not blame the United States or the West or modernity for all the problems in the Muslim World. They recognize that the decline of the Islamic civilization preceded colonialism. They are aware that the decay of free and creative thinking in the Muslim World was not caused by Western powers but came about as a result of internal dynamics. Moderate Muslims are critical of the polemics against the West, the rising anti-Semitism, and the tendency to blame Israel for everything problematic in the Muslim World and the growing intolerance, sectarianism, and authoritarianism in Muslim societies. Above all they lament the intellectual decline of the Muslim World.

Moderate Muslims are also engaged in what is now referred to as the "battle for the soul of Islam." They argue that Islam is a message of compassion and peace sent by God to civilize humanity and give human existence a transcendent and divine purpose. They are aghast and reject the use of Islam to incite terror, to justify bigotry, and to discriminate on the basis of faith or gender or ethnicity. They recognize that Islam has been appropriated by political and extremist groups who are using Islam as an ideology to pursue a counter-hegemonic agenda both with the Muslim World and against the rest, especially against the United States. Moderate Muslims acknowledge the global problem created by rogue Islamists. They insist that the false interpretations of Islam by the *jihadi*s and their crusades not only are creating a global *fitna* (crisis) but also are corrupting the essence of Islam and worsening the sociopolitical, economic, and cultural crisis in the Muslim World.

The United States and liberal Islam share a common strategic goal in the battle for the soul of Islam: the systematic dismantling and delegitimization of the discourse coming from rogue Islamists that projects America as an anti-Islam crusader power and Islam as an ideology of hate and violence. The war on terror will be won or lost in the arena of interpretation and reinterpretation of global political realities and religious texts and their contemporaneous meanings. It is also in this contested realm that the hearts and minds of Muslims can be won or lost. While moderate Muslims are beginning to have an impact on this battle in America, so far they are not even an important player in the Muslim World. American policymakers must recognize the strategic value of liberal Islam and promote and protect it.

WHAT ROLE CAN MODERATE MUSLIMS PLAY IN THE WAR ON TERROR?

Moderate Muslims have an enormous potential to become an important ally in America's war against extremism. If consulted and brought into counterterrorism planning, they can help the United States become more effective, more focused, and more cost effective. They can and could have played a major role in the following areas.

Provide a Muslim Face to America

Moderate Muslims could have given a Muslim face to America's response to September 11, thus averting the feeling in the Muslim World that this is a Christian-Zionist crusade against Islam. The Bush administration should have appointed a number of prominent moderate Muslim athletes, such as Hakeem Olajuwon, and some imams such as Imam Hamza Yusuf (an American convert to Islam who is well respected in the Muslim World) as special envoys of goodwill. The State Department is now attempting this in a less notable way. A prominent Muslim presence in America's diplomatic and counterterrorism endeavors would have gone a long way not only in preempting the rise of anti-Americanism but also in building trust between the United States and the Muslim World.

Provide Human Intelligence

Some of the most important assets that moderate Muslims can bring to the war on terror are human intelligence, cultural insights, linguistic skills and experience, and awareness of the diversity within Islamic groups and movements. It is possible that the Federal Bureau of Investigation (FBI), the Central Intelligence Agency (CIA), and the National Security Agency (NSA) can access this resource through recruitment. But voluntary support in this area from the community can be priceless.

Many moderate Muslim scholars have argued that Islam and democracy are compatible. The Bush administration could have recruited several of them to make this case in Iraq and help design the Iraqi democracy and write its constitution. Without a significant input from respectable Muslim scholars, the Iraqi constitution may not stand up to accusations that it is un-Islamic and written to make Iraq subservient to U.S. interests. Moderate Muslims opposed to extremism can also play a role in undercover operations like that played by Mubin Sheikh in Canada and in the Showtime series *Sleeper Cell.*

Counter Radical Islamic Discourse

One important arena in which the United States needs its Muslim citizens is in countering the anti-U.S. propaganda. Both Islamists and governmental media have launched a propaganda war against the United States in response to its war on terror. This anti-U.S. media offensive is determined to focus on American foreign policy excesses and failures. It also seeks to explain every aspect of American policy as if it is serving only Israeli interests. With moderate Muslims as spokespersons surfing the media and the airwaves in the Muslim World, the United States would have a better chance of getting a more balanced view of its policies.

Moderate Muslims can also counter the abuse of Islam by rogue Islamists and undermine their legitimacy. Moderate Muslim scholars have consistently maintained that hirabah (terrorism) is not jihad and is strictly prohibited by Islamic principles. They have also demonstrated how suicide bombings violate Islamic ethics of self-defense and are not legitimate instruments of jihad. If their voices were given more attention (say through a White House–sponsored conference on jihad), many of the moderate and liberal elements in the Muslim World would recognize the fallacies in the Islamic edicts of rogue Islamists and the scholars who support and justify their cause.

Moderate Muslims can provide an alternative understanding of political and global realities to prevent the perception that the war on terror is a war on Islam. They could advance a liberal understanding of religion within the Islamic idiom that explains the compatibility of Islam and liberal values such as tolerance, democracy, and pluralism. Scholars could also deconstruct the jihadis' discourse to expose the extremist tendencies behind their interpretation of Islam and underscore the more compassionate and rational dimensions of Islam.

Restore Balance to America's Foreign Policy

To put it bluntly, U.S. foreign policy under George W. Bush is a colossal failure and even potentially dangerous to America's interests. This administration would do well to listen to some moderate Muslim voices in shaping its foreign policy objectives and in determining tactics. Except for the case of Israel, moderate Muslims have the same vision for the Muslim World that this administration claims to have. Moderate Muslims also want wholesale regime changes and establishment of democracy in the entire Muslim World. They too want to see the general human rights environment improving and wish that prosperity and freedom would take root there. The difference is that moderate Muslims would recommend strategies that are more humane and do not involve wars and invasions, torture, and violation of civil rights. This administration needs moderate Muslims: the time has come for it to act on this need and include them in its policy deliberations.

The Structure of the Debate

In this book, which is based on a special issue of the *American Journal of Islamic Social Sciences* (Fall 2005), prominent voices from the policy community, the academic community, and the American Muslim community come together to debate who is a moderate Muslim and just what moderation means in a theological as well as a geopolitical sense. The participants also debate and reflect on the future of political Islam, the role of Islam in Muslim politics, Western policies in the Muslim World and their ramifications, and, finally, the future of American-Muslim relations.

Given that the structure of this debate is a bit unusual and complex, I feel that it is important to explain it. There are two types of participants: the actual debaters and the commentators. The debaters (Ariel Cohen, John L. Esposito, Graham E. Fuller, Abid Ullah Jan, and M. A. Muqtedar Khan) make two contributions: each one answers the same five related questions and then rebuts and responds to the answers provided by the other four participants.

Each participant brings a wide range of perspectives to this debate. Cohen is a prominent policy analyst at a prestigious think-tank associated with a strongly conservative and occasionally neoconservative viewpoint. Esposito is a widely respected and quoted authority on Islam and an important voice in the academy. Fuller is a former intelligence analyst who brings both sensitivity to the government's viewpoint and an awareness of security and geopolitical issues. Jan, who is associated with the Islamic movement in Pakistan, is representative of what is known as political Islamism. Khan, the convener and editor of this debate, is often referred to as the voice of moderate Islam. The participants expose the enormous complexity of the issues at hand and manifest the great diversity of views and interpretations in the ongoing discussion of American-Islamic relations.

The commentators are Feisal Rauf, Ali Mazrui, Louay Safi, Mahmood Mamdani, Hakan Yavuz, and Taha Jabir al-Alwani. Feisal Rauf is a prominent Muslim in New York who speaks from a Sufi and traditional Islamic perspective. Ali Mazrui is a well-known scholar of African studies and U.S.-Muslim global relations who offers a strong critical perspective. Louay Safi is a prominent American Muslim leader and scholar who represents the mainstream U.S. Muslim view on the subject. Mahmood Mamdani is an anthropologist who is very critical of U.S. foreign policy toward the Third World and suspicious of the very idea of identifying Muslims as moderate and radical. Hakan Yavuz, of Turkish heritage, is an expert on Islam and the politics of Turkey who adds a political science perspective. Taha Jabir al-Alwani is a preeminent jurist who brings the *fiqhi* or Islamic juristic view to the debate.

These contributors, who enjoy a great deal of freedom, were asked to comment on the debate itself or to answer the questions, if they felt that the debaters were missing some vital issues. Their perspectives are wide and deep, for they look at the issues from jurisprudential, mystical, anthropological, progressive, and political standpoints. The commentaries on the debate are followed by "The Last Word." Kamran Bokhari and Farid Senzai offer the combined perspective of security studies and international relations. Islamic studies scholar Asma Afsaruddin adds a much-needed Muslim woman scholar's perspective to the debate on contemporary geopolitics.

Those who are academically interested in Islam's role in global politics will discover a great deal of material in this debate. Policymakers will find many issues clarified as well as clear directions for improving American-Muslim relations and combating extremism. Many of the ideas and analyses presented herein will stimulate debate and understanding.

QUESTIONS ASKED IN THE DEBATE

The following questions were asked of each debater. They are repeated in abbreviated form in each chapter of the debate.

[**QUESTION 1**] *Commentators have frequently invoked the importance of moderate Muslims and the role that they can play in fighting extremism in the Muslim World. But it is not clear who is a moderate Muslim. The recent cancellation of Tariq Ramadan's visa to the United States, the raids on several American Muslim organizations, and the near marginalization of mainstream Muslims in North America raise the following question: If moderate Muslims are critical to an American victory in the war on terror, why does the U.S. government frequently take steps that undermine moderate Muslims? Perhaps it is not clear who the moderate Muslims are. In* *your view, who are these moderate Muslims and what are their beliefs and politics?*

[**QUESTION 2**] *The Muslim World is experiencing a period of turmoil. At its heart is the debate over the role of Islam in Muslim society, particularly in its political sphere. At one extreme is secular despotism, which seeks to dominate Muslim societies; and at the other extreme is the specter of Islamic totalitarianism. The hope in the middle is the possible role that moderate Muslims can play in establishing Islamic democracies. Theorists in the West have visualized secular Turkey as a model for the Muslim World. Is it possible to imagine that the Turkish Islamists, now under the leadership of visionaries such as Prime Minister Tayyip Erdogan, are the harbingers of moderate Islam and Islamic democracy?*

[**QUESTION 3**] *Moderate Muslims are often associated with their advocacy of ijtihad (independent thinking) and the subsequent reform of Muslim practice and interpretation of Islam through its much wider and systematic revival and application. Do you think that this faith in the promise of ijtihad is justified? Where is reform necessary? What do you understand by the term "Islamic reform"? Can Muslims develop modern, democratic, and prosperous societies without abandoning the wisdom and blessings of revelation?*

[**QUESTION 4**] *What is the future of political Islam? Does the emergence of radical groups such as al-Qaeda and others undermine the legitimacy of Islamic movements in the Muslim World or enhance their appeal? Will we witness resurgence in the relevance and influence of groups such as the Jamaat-i Islami and the Ikhwan al-Muslimeen, or will they slowly lose ground to more moderate movements? Will political Islamic movements radicalize or democratize?*

[**QUESTION 5**] *The growing presence of Islam in the West has clearly reached strategic proportions. Transatlantic relations are being mediated by the strength of Muslim minorities in Europe. North America has a growing and influential Muslim community. Some scholars and experts see Islam in the West as a threat, while others see it as a potential bridge between the West and the Muslim World. What impact will Islam have on the West and on Islamic-Western relations? Is the future of Islam and Muslims in the West in danger?*

{ II }

THE DEBATE

Chapter 2

POWER OR IDEOLOGY
What Islamists Choose Will
Determine Their Future

ARIEL COHEN

[**QUESTION 1**] *If moderate Muslims are critical to an American victory in the war on terror, why does the U.S. government frequently take steps that undermine moderate Muslims? In your view, who are these moderate Muslims and what are their beliefs and politics?*

ARIEL COHEN (AC): I would like to say from the outset that I am neither a Muslim nor a sociologist. Therefore, my remarks should be taken as those of an interested and sympathetic outsider.

I do not believe at all that the American government "undermines" moderate Muslims. The problem is more complicated. Many U.S. officials abhor engagement with religion or the politics of religion. They believe that the American Constitution separates religion and state and does not allow them to make distinctions when it comes to different interpretations of Islam. For some of them, Salafi Islam is as good as Sufi Islam.

Others do not have a sufficient knowledge base to sort out the moderates from the radicals, identify the retrograde fundamentalists, or recognize modernizers who want political Islam to dominate. This is wrong. Radical ideologies have to do more with politics and warfare than with religion and, in some extreme cases, should not enjoy the constitutional protections of freedom of religion or free speech. There is a difference between propagating a faith and disseminating hatred, violence, or murder. The latter is an abuse and exploitation of faith for political ends and should be treated as such. For example, the racist Aryan Nation churches were prosecuted and bankrupted by American nongovernment organizations (NGOs) and the U.S. government.

One of the problems is that the American government allows radical Muslims who support terrorism to operate with impunity in the United States and around the world and does very little to support moderate Muslims, especially in the conflict zones. To me, moderate Muslims are those who do not view the greater jihad either as a pillar of faith or as a predominant dimension thereof. A moderate is one who is searching for a dialogue and a compromise with people who adhere to other interpretations of the Qur'an and with those who are not Muslim. A moderate Sunni, for example, will not support terror attacks on Shia or Sufis or on Christians, Jews, or Hindus.

Moderate Muslims respect the right of individuals to disagree, to worship Allah in the way they choose or not to worship—and even not to believe. A moderate Muslim is one who is willing to bring his or her brother or sister to faith by love and logic, not by mortal threats or force of arms. A moderate Muslim decries suicide bombings and terrorist "operations" and abhors those clerics who indoctrinate toward, bless, and support such atrocities.

The list of moderate Muslims is too long to give all or even part of it here. Sheikh Muhammad Hisham Kabbani (chairman of the Islamic Supreme Council of America) and Sheikh Abdul Hadi Palazzi (secretary-general of the Rome-based Italian Muslim Association) come to mind. Ayatollah Ali Sistani may be a moderate, but I need to read more of his teachings. As the Wahhabi attacks against the Shia escalate, Shia clerics and leaders are beginning to speak up. Examples include Sheikh Agha Jafri, a Westchester-based Pakistani Shia who heads an organization called the Society for Humanity and Islam in America (on the Internet he is listed as spokesman for the Universal Muslim Association of America), and Tashbih Sayyed, a California-based Pakistani who serves as president of the Council for Democracy and Tolerance.

I admire the bravery of Amina Wadud, a female professor of Islamic studies at Virginia Commonwealth University who led a mixed-gender Friday Islamic prayer service.[1] Another brave woman is the co-founder of the Progressive Muslim Union of America, Sarah Eltantawi. And the whole world is proud of the achievements of Judge Shirin Ebadi, the Iranian human rights lawyer who was awarded the Nobel peace prize in 2003.

There is a problem with the first question, however. It contains several assumptions that are debatable, to say the least, if not outright false. First, it assumes that Tariq Ramadan is a "moderate." Nevertheless, there is near consensus that Ramadan, while calling for ijtihad, is a supporter of the Egyptian Ikhwan al-Muslimeen and comes from that tradition (he is the grandson of its founder, Hassan al-Banna). He also expressed support for Yusuf al-Qaradawi (and all he stands for) on a British Broadcasting Corporation (BBC) television program and is viewed as an anti-Semite. Ramadan rationalizes the murder of children, though that apparently did not preclude the European Social Forum from inviting him to be a member. He has exchanged compliments with Hassan al-Turabi, the founder of the Islamic state in Sudan. Numerous reports in the media, quoting intelligence sources and ex-terrorists, indicate that Ramadan associates with the most radical circles, including terrorists. In its decision to ban him, the United States Department of Homeland Security was guided by a number of issues, some of them reported in the media and others classified. This is sufficient for me to believe that Ramadan may be a security risk who could reasonably be banned from entering the United States in the post-9/11 environment.[2]

Second, the raids on "American Muslim organizations" are in fact a part of law enforcement operations. Some of these steps had to do with investigations of terrorist activities, such as the alleged Libyan conspiracy to assassinate Crown Prince Abdullah of Saudi Arabia. Others focused on American Islamist organizations that funded the terrorist activities of groups on the State Department's terrorism watch list, such as Hamas. To say that these criminal investigations are targeting moderate Islam is like saying that investigating pedophile priests undermines freedom of religion in the United States.

Finally, American Muslims are hardly marginalized. They enjoy unencumbered religious life and support numerous nongovernmental organizations, which often take positions highly critical of domestic and foreign policy—something that is often not the case in their countries of origin. There is no job discrimination: some senior Bush administration officials, such as Elias A. Zerhouni, head of the National Institutes of Health (NIH), are Muslims. American presidents have congratulated Muslims on religious holidays and often invite Muslim clergy to important state functions, such as the funeral of President Ronald Reagan.

[**QUESTION 2**] *Is it possible to imagine that the Turkish Islamists, now under the leadership of visionaries such as Prime Minister Erdogan, are the harbingers of moderate Islam and Islamic democracy?*

AC: The Turkish case is country- and society-specific. When the Turkish Islamic politicians talk to Westerners, they call themselves "Turkish Christian Democrats"—culturally conservative, economically market-oriented, and open to the outside world. Internally, they promote agendas that raise eyebrows in the West and raise hackles among Turkish secularists, such as increased funding for secondary religious education, preferential treatment for the graduates of religious schools in college admissions, criminalizing adultery, and relaxing rules on the hijab (women's head scarf).

The core constituency of the AK (Justice and Development) Party is less than 20 percent of the Turkish electorate. The rest are opportunists who voted for the Islamic party because of nonreligious issues, such as its promises of more effective and less corrupt governance. They may swing away from the AK Party, as they have from other Turkish parties in the past. In other countries, the ratio of core voters and fellow travelers can be different, affecting the strength of Islamists in power.

Historically, Ottoman Islam was rather tolerant, especially during the centuries when the caliphate was in decline. The millet system, in which Christians and Jews were treated as autonomous communities, is a far cry from what is happening in many Muslim states today. The relationship between Islam and the state had been evolving for centuries in the Ottoman Empire, until Mustafa Kemal Atatürk made a harsh break and essentially introduced the separation of mosque and state. Although the evolutionary pendulum may now be swinging in the opposite direction, the Turkish state still works along the lines of a secular constitution. In other places where Islamists participate in politics, this may or may not be the case.

Today the AK Party's version of the relationship between mosque and state is considerably more flexible than some of the modern interpretations in Iran (*vilayat-i faqih*), Pakistan (the Jamaat-i Islami), Saudi Arabia (the Salafists), or the Maghreb (the Islamic Salvation Front [FIS]). Moreover, if Turkey engages in the process of integrating into the European Union, a lot of issues between mosque and state will be influenced and regulated by the documents defining accession, the so-called *acquis communautaire*. Separation of mosque and state, just like separation of church and state, will be a part of such regulation. Limits will also be placed upon the political, governmental, and social agendas promoted by Islamists.

The political participation of Islamic parties in democratic societies is quite feasible and is happening beyond Turkey. This has been demonstrated in Bangladesh, Indonesia, Malaysia, Pakistan, Tajikistan, and elsewhere. Each country and each society has its own history and political constellation. If constitutions are adhered to, and if they stipulate essentially non–Shariah based state architectures, Islamic parties will be capable of playing in the political field without breaking the constitutional sandbox.

[**QUESTION 3**] *Do you think that faith in the promise of ijtihad is justified? Where is reform necessary? What do you understand by the term "Islamic reform"? Can Muslims develop modern, democratic, and prosperous societies without abandoning the wisdom and blessings of revelation?*

AC: My understanding is that ijtihad is recognized by the Shia and frowned upon by mainstream scholars in the four principal Sunni madhhabs (legal schools). The world is changing, however, and the way we deal with it needs to keep up with the times. This is the essence of social evolution and reform. The lack of ability to evolve leads to dead ends in faith, politics, and economics. I do not wish this fate for anyone, including my Muslim friends. But abandoning values, ethics, and religion makes the modern techno-driven world soulless and dangerous. The challenge is to find the golden mean. Every religion, every culture, finds a different answer.

The modern world is more interconnected, business knows no national borders, and large corporations are global. Many new technological breakthroughs need to be adjusted to our lives. Or we need to adjust to new technologies. The notion of modernization needs to be reconciled with faith. Religion has a place for innovation, which makes societies more modern and their members happier. If Muslims feel that their religion is too oppressive, many will leave it in disappointment.

The key to innovation is the ability to interpret the sacred text in such a way that it lives in harmony with our times. The text may require reinterpretation to accomplish that. Bringing women to equality is a huge challenge in Islam. Treating non-Muslims as equals and with respect, within the land of Islam and outside, is another critical challenge. Various branches of any religion may emphasize different parts of the sacred texts, thereby developing divergent narratives. After all, the Qur'an and the *hadith* were written for a time and place very different from today. For example, the marriage age was quite different—none but the strictest of literal fundamentalists would agree with marrying off nine-year-old girls nowadays, even if that was the age of the Prophet's youngest wife. Women did not drive, because cars did not exist. They did not go to college, because there were no colleges. Maybe the ancient societies could afford not to have women in the workforce or to keep them segregated; but this is too high a price to pay in today's world, and it is impoverishing the land of Islam, by its own reports.

Many ancient Middle Eastern societies were tribal, monoethnic, and religiously intolerant. Conquering and assimilating "the other" was the norm. This was quite different from the mega-cities of the planet today. Religious intolerance and rejection of others, as well as their values and even their right to exist, are quickly becoming a defining feature of the more intolerant wings in the Muslim World, however. This is where the reform is urgent—and probably overdue.

The sacred texts must remain spiritually relevant but may mean different things to various people in different periods. Ijtihad does not take away the wisdom and beauty of the revelation. I am sure that the Old and New Testaments meant different things in the ancient Middle East, when these books were given—or written—and in medieval Europe. Modern interpretations are viewed through yet another new prism. This is why divergent commentaries and interpretations, from Thomas Aquinas (d. 1274) to Moses Maimonides (d. 1204), to Ibn Rushd (d. 1198), to Reinhold Niebuhr (d. 1971), have proliferated. The three monotheistic religions influenced each other, including the inspiration of Sufi Islam for some of the mystical teachings of both Judaism and Christianity. Why not explore lessons from the evolution of these two religions in a quest toward developing more tolerant interpretations that embrace modernity?

In ancient times Judaism and Christianity were far more intolerant religions than they are now. But they evolved. Those who reject modernity (including some aspects of technology), like the ultra-Orthodox Jews and the Amish in the United States, are marginalized. They have become sects of their own respective faiths. Muslims who reject technology, modernity, and progress, like the Taliban, are probably turning into blind alleys of human development. Furthermore, because the world is a more crowded place with evolving norms of behavior, the "old ways," which often resulted in warfare, may need to be reexamined and adjusted. With people inventing weapons that may end civilization as we know it, some previous pronouncements regarding the killing of infidels may need to be reviewed and revised.

The world recognizes human equality, including gender equality, and the rights of ethnic and religious minorities as central elements of today's existence. Religions need to come to grips with this. Other faiths already have: the Christian Reformation in the late Middle Ages, the Vatican II reforms of the 1960s, the emergence of Haskala (Education/Enlightenment) in eighteenth-century Orthodox Judaism and of the non-Orthodox (Conservative, Reform, and Reconstructionist) branches of Judaism in the nineteenth and twentieth centuries. Jewish modern Orthodoxy emerged in the last century. These reforms in the two other great religions of the People of the Book addressed specific needs and enriched the fabric of these faiths without destroying their divine origins. The need to adjust may affect most interpretations of Islam—otherwise, serious contradictions within Islamic societies (such as the rights of women or the desire to be and feel a part of the outside world) will continue to expand. Is there a better tool to deal with conflicts and contradictions than ijtihad?

The Iranian example demonstrates that ijtihad by itself may not be sufficient. Too often, religion is used in conjunction with politics or for political ends. Thus ijtihad may need to be explored in parallel with clear notions of separation of religion and state, moving the faith into the realm of the spiritual and personal and away from politics and the temptations of state. Then and only then can Muslims have the opportunity to create prosperous, modern, and democratic societies.

[**QUESTION 4**] *What is the future of political Islam? Does the emergence of radical groups undermine the legitimacy of Islamic movements in the Muslim World or enhance their appeal? Will we witness a resurgence in the relevance and influence of groups such as the Jamaat-i Islami and the Ikhwan al-Muslimeen, or will they slowly lose ground to more moderate movements? Will political Islamic movements radicalize or democratize?*

ac: The Jewish sages said that after the destruction of the Temple of Jerusalem the gift of prophecy was given to fools. So I would rather not prophesy. The future of political Islam is what it makes of itself. If it pursues the road of violence, it will be met with violence, possibly with overwhelming force, including force from within the Muslim World. In the short run an escalation in fighting may bring new proponents to its ranks. But in the long run radical, violent Islam will be hounded, denied sources of funding, and isolated, just as the Kharijites (an early Islamic militant sect) were.

Moreover, the three state-sized experiments of political Islam (Iran, Afghanistan, and Sudan) are seen as unappealing at best and as hellish failures at worst—not only by the outside world but also by the majority of Muslims. People vote with their feet. More people want to live in the United States and Western Europe than in Afghanistan, Iran, and Sudan under their respective Islamic regimes. Similarly, more people wanted to live in West Germany, Taiwan, and South Korea than in East Germany, China, and North Korea. You cannot fool all of the people all of the time, and it is not accidental that films and books concerning Afghanistan under the Taliban produced by Afghans themselves depict a nightmare world of oppression and cruelty.

Finally, a lot will depend on mass support for political Islam. How determined and committed will it be? How effective will the West, moderate Muslims, and governments throughout the Greater Middle East be in demonstrating the political and moral bankruptcy of violent movements and their leaders? For example, what about the hundreds of millions of dollars that radical Muslim leaders either received from the Saudi royal family, whom they now decry, or "earned" through drug sales and diamond trafficking? Why do Islamist leaders, so quick to rationalize acts of martyrdom, not send their own children to commit murder-suicide bombings or just go push the buttons themselves?

As for legitimacy, a lot depends on the West as well. Failure delegitimizes. A failure in the self-professed service of God (Allah) delegitimizes completely. With no military wins, al-Qaeda and its allies may suffer a loss of popular support. The Jamaat-i Islami and the Ikhwan al-Muslimeen are more complicated cases, because their success depends on the failure of secular dictatorial opponents. If the government of Egypt, for example, opens the political space for reforms and voters see results, the Ikhwan may lose support. The Ikhwan al-Muslimeen, Hamas, and Hizbollah show a lot of tactical flexibility, however, by reaching out to individuals and circles traditionally not in their camp in order to broaden their support.

The test for some of these movements is what they value more: power or ideology. If it is power, they may compromise and liberalize in the democratic context or may try for a violent solution, such as a coup—and if they do, they are likely to fail. If ideology is more important, they will remain rigid and may decline like the Western European Communists did.

[QUESTION 5] *What impact will Islam have on the West and on Islamic-Western relations? Is the future of Islam and Muslims in the West in danger?*

AC: We cannot talk about the Muslim "community" as a whole. There are different communities with divergent agendas. Some want to be Westerners of Islamic faith, enjoying economic opportunities and an essentially Western lifestyle. Others are Muslims who happen to live in the West and view the United States, and especially Europe, as simply additional places that must be "Islamized." Some of the Saudi-funded curricula in Western Muslim schools speak for themselves, when they preach hatred of the "infidels."

European positions on the Middle East have evolved as the Muslim minorities there have grown. This may explain, in part, the French opposition to the Iraq war. The murder of individual activists, however, like the public slaughter of filmmaker Theo van Gogh in Holland in 2004, or sustained support for terrorism may bring on a backlash against Muslims in Europe.

Those who view Muslims as a threat point to their low rate of integration in European societies. European racism and cultural rigidity probably are partially to blame for this. But some practices of Islam in Europe give ample reason for Europeans to be nervous. Many Europeans view radical Muslims' social norms of women's inequality, polygamy, and religious intolerance as threatening the core values of European secularist culture. The phenomenon of "weekend imams" who fly in from the Middle East to preach and leave after spending a weekend in the "land of infidels" worries not just European governments but local moderate Muslims as well. Human rights norms and laws designed for more peaceful times prevent police departments in Europe from actively pursuing those who plan attacks on government buildings and civilian targets in Great Britain, France, Spain, and elsewhere, although this is slowly changing.

Americans are more tolerant of people of different faiths and races than their European cousins are. In the past, the United States successfully absorbed immigrants from Asia, Eastern Europe, and the Middle East. Nonetheless, the domination of Wahhabi preachers in the majority of U.S. mosques and support of terrorist organizations could undermine the tolerance of the American masses and body politic for the peaceful life of Muslims in this country. If another massive terror attack happens in the United States, one cannot vouch for the reaction of the public and the state. But even then such self-defense would probably be exercised within the confines of the Constitution and according to the rule of law.

Moderate Islam, which cleanses itself of extremism, may be a bridge to integration and a form of faith that promotes tolerance and allows Islam to thrive in Western societies. For that to happen, Islam at large—including those influential *ulama* with access to massive petro-dollar financial support—needs to make adjustments. For example, those ulama need to start isolating and decrying radicals and terrorists and actively pursuing genuine peaceful political solutions for conflicts in the Greater Middle East, including Israel and its neighbors and Iraq. Such solutions would recognize the rights of all the region's states, minority groups, and inhabitants to a peaceful life with dignity and security.

Finally, to survive and succeed in the West and throughout the Muslim World, Islamic leaders and elites need to revisit and reexamine their social agendas. They need to recognize and secure women's rights; face the changing nature of gender relations; acknowledge the necessity to promote secular education, including education for women and girls; and work to promote family planning and limit high birth rates, which only breed poverty and social failure. When progress is achieved on these diverse and complex agendas, the future of Islam will be more secure.

Notes

1. Mona Eltahawy, "A Prayer toward Equality," *Washington Post,* March 18, 2005.

2. http://www.militantislammonitor.org/article/id/255.

Chapter 3

MODERATE MUSLIMS

A Mainstream of Modernists, Islamists, Conservatives, and Traditionalists

JOHN L. ESPOSITO

[**QUESTION 1**] *If moderate Muslims are critical to an American victory in the war on terror, why does the U.S. government frequently take steps that undermine moderate Muslims? In your view, who are these moderate Muslims and what are their beliefs and politics?*

JOHN L. ESPOSITO (JLE): Our human tendency is to define what is normal or moderate in terms of someone just like "us." The American government, many Western and Muslim governments, and experts define moderate by searching for reflections of themselves. Thus Irshad Manji or "secular" Muslims are singled out as self-critical moderate Muslims by such diverse commentators as Thomas Friedman and Daniel Pipes. In an America that is politicized by the Republican Party and the religious Right after 9/11 and by the association of Islam with global terrorism, defining a moderate Muslim becomes even more problematic. Look at the situations not only in the United States but also in Europe, especially France. Is a moderate Muslim one who accepts integration, or must it be assimilation? Is a moderate Muslim secular, as in laic (which is really antireligious)? Is a moderate Muslim one who accepts secularism, as in separation of church and state, so that no religion is privileged and the rights of all (believer and nonbeliever) are protected? Is a moderate Muslim one who accepts a particular notion of gender relations, not simply the equality of women and men but a position against wearing a hijab? (Let us not forget, of course, that we have an analogous problem with many Muslims whose definition of being a Muslim or of being a "good" Muslim woman is as narrowly defined.)

In today's climate, defining who is a moderate Muslim depends on the politics or religious positions of the individuals making the judgment: Bernard Lewis, Daniel Pipes, Gilles Kepel, Stephen Schwartz, Pat Robertson, and Tom DeLay. The extent to which things have gotten out of hand is seen in attempts to define moderate Islam or what it means to be a good European or American Muslim. France has defined the meaning of moderate Muslim and being French, sought to influence mosques, and legislated against wearing the hijab in schools. Non-Muslim individuals and organizations in the United States, as well as the government, establish or fund organizations that define or promote "moderate Islam" and Islamic pluralism as well as monitor mainstream mosques and organizations. The influence of foreign policy plays a critical role. For some, if not many, the litmus test for a moderate Muslim is tied to foreign policy issues: for example, how critical people are of American or French policy or their position in regard to Palestine/Israel, Algeria, Kashmir, and Iraq.

Like many Muslim regimes, many experts and ideologues as well as publications like the *Weekly Standard, National Review, Atlantic,* and *New York Sun* and media like Fox Television portray all Islamists as being the same. Mainstream or extremist (they deny any distinction between the two), all Muslims who do not completely accept their notion of secularism—the absolute separation of religion and the state—are regarded as a threat. Mainstream Islamists or other Islamically oriented voices are dismissed as "wolves in sheep's clothing." It is important to emphasize that these people not only have influence and an impact as individual personalities: their ideas have taken on a life of their own and become part of popular culture. In a post-9/11 climate they reinforce the worst fears of the uninformed.

The term "moderate" is in many ways deceptive. It can be used in juxtaposition with "extremist" and can imply that someone has to be a liberal reformer or a progressive in order to pass the moderate test, thus excluding more conservative or traditionalist positions. Moderates in Islam, as in all faiths, are the majority or mainstream. We assume this in regard to other faiths such as Judaism and Christianity. The Muslim mainstream itself represents a multitude of religious and socioeconomic positions. Minimally, moderate Muslims are those who live and work "within" societies, seek change from below, reject religious extremism, and consider violence and terrorism to be illegitimate. Often, in differing ways, they interpret and reinterpret Islam to respond more effectively to the religious, social, and political realities of their societies and to international affairs.

Some seek to Islamize their societies but eschew political Islam; others do not.

Moderate Muslims constitute a broad spectrum politically, ranging from those who wish to see more Islamically oriented states to "Muslim Democrats," comparable to Europe's Christian Democrats. The point here, as in other faiths, is that the moderate mainstream is a very diverse and disparate group of people who can, in religious and political terms, span the spectrum from conservatives to liberal reformers. They may disagree or agree on many matters. Moderate Jews and Christians can hold positions ranging from reform to ultra-Orthodox and fundamentalist and at times can bitterly disagree on theological and social policies (such as gay rights, abortion, the ordination of women, and American foreign and domestic policies). So can moderate Muslims.

[**QUESTION 2**] *Is it possible to imagine that the Turkish Islamists, now under the leadership of visionaries such as Prime Minister Erdogan, are the harbingers of moderate Islam and Islamic democracy?*

JLE: Turkey simply constitutes one possible contemporary example or experiment. It may prove to be a model for some, but certainly not for all. Democratization in the Muslim World can take many forms (just as Islamic states or republics can take many forms). Indonesia, Turkey, Malaysia, and others represent "diverse works in progress." Ultimately, while new forms of Muslim democracies may share basic principles and values (as do many democracies in the West), the specific form will be influenced by and respond to local (national and regional) realities—religious, ethnic, tribal, cultural, and linguistic. Anyone who has traveled in the Muslim World has experienced the distinct political and cultural differences between Sudan and Bangladesh, between Saudi Arabia and Yemen, or between Egypt and Indonesia. Despite diverse historical and political experiences, we see in many parts of the Muslim World a call for more political participation, the rule of law, human rights, and less authoritarianism, concentration of power, oppression, and corruption.

The paths chosen in these diverse societies, while they have similar endpoints, will differ and reflect local conditions and accommodations. Good examples of the diversity of experiences today are Egypt, Bahrain, Iraq, Pakistan, and Indonesia, in terms of both democratic forces and government responses or policies, which range from control and repression to cautious limited democratization. The critical issue today is whether domestic and international conditions will enable individual Muslim countries to move beyond the culture and values of authoritarianism represented and perpetuated by secular despotism and Islamic totalitarianism. Here the international community can play an important role. The United States and Europe, in particular, have potentially important roles to play in everything from economic and educational development to support for developing strong civil societies and democratic institutions.

[QUESTION 3] *Do you think that faith in the promise of ijtihad is justified? Where is reform necessary? What do you understand by the term "Islamic reform"? Can Muslims develop modern, democratic, andprosperous societies without abandoning the wisdom and blessings of revelation?*

JLE: Historically, Islam, like all religious faiths, has developed as a result of a process of interpretation and reinterpretation. Religious traditions are the product of sacred texts and contexts, the word of God or scriptures interpreted and applied by human beings in specific historical and social contexts. The degree of change may vary (from conservative to more reformist) historically, but the process has always been there. I would emphasize here that the phrase "moderate Muslim" should not be measured by how reformist a Muslim is. Moderates, as I noted above, come in all shapes.

The process of ijtihad, especially if it includes incorporating subsidiary legal principles such as equity (*istihsan*) and the general welfare or public interest (*maslahah*), can be a powerful instrument for reform. The form of ijtihad that many will increasingly turn to, however, goes beyond the tendency in the past to restrict ijtihad to analogical reasoning (*qiyas*) in order to limit the diversity of opinion.

A primary and critical issue today is "Whose Islam?" Who is to interpret, who is qualified? As in the past, some rulers are only too happy to do so; and, of course, many of the ulama see the law and its interpretation as their sole task. Defining or understanding who is qualified to engage in ijtihad must, as some Muslims contend, be broadened beyond the traditional notion of the ulama to all people whose expertise has a bearing on the practice of ijtihad. It is often said that Islam has no clergy (this is certainly the case in Sunni Islam). Neither the Qur'an nor the Prophet Muhammad created a clergy. Yet, in fact, the ulama emerged as a self-perpetuating class and clergy—and many wish to keep it that way. Many of the issues in reform, however, require a multidisciplinary expertise and approach in the areas of science, politics, economics, and international affairs. Similarly, as many Muslims in the recent past and today have contended, the implementation of the results of ijtihad and consensus (*ijma'*) can be transferred from or shared by rulers, the ulama, lay experts, and parliaments.

Islam has a long modernist or reformist legacy to be drawn on today. Remember that the call for modern reform, for ijtihad, is over a century old. It is instructive to look back to the time of Muhammad Abduh (d. 1905) and Muhammad Iqbal (d. 1938). What Iqbal and others said decades ago still resonates today: Islam has been static for more than five hundred years and needs a reformation. Like other Islamic modernists, Iqbal rejected much of classical or medieval Islam as stagnant, part of the problem rather than part of the solution. He saw Islam as emerging from five hundred years of "dogmatic slumber" and compared the need for Islamic reform to the Reformation (*The Reconstruction of Religious Thought in Islam* [London: Oxford University Press, 1934], chapter 6): "We are today passing through a period similar to that of the Protestant Reformation in Europe and the lesson which the rise and outcome of Luther's movement teaches should not be lost on us."

Although Iqbal's comparison with the Protestant Reformation refers to the need for a process of reform, this should not prejudge the actual shape that those reforms might take. I would also remind us all that the Reformation, like all reformations, was not just about an "enlightenment." The process included heat as well as light, violence as well as insight, plus the marginalization and persecution of reformers. The Reformation involved not only theological debate and differences but also religious wars followed by a Counter-Reformation.

While times have changed, many of the principles of Islamic modernism remain significant. A central principle is the need to distinguish between divine laws and principles and human interpretations, between regulations concerning worship or duties to God (*'ibadat*) that cannot change and social regulations (*mu'amalat*) that can be changed. We also need to remember that while many of the ideas of reformers such as Abduh and Iqbal were important, the project did not take hold, due to existing political, economic, and social conditions. In particular, the toughest nut to crack in most attempts at religious reform is the conservative religious establishment's firm grip on the training of religious leaders and on religious discourse, doctrine, and practice. In Islam, this means the ulama, *madrassah*s (institutions of learning, usually used for schools), and mosques and their Islamic discourses.

Finally, there is no reason why Muslims cannot develop modern, prosperous democratic societies while still retaining their faith and identity. In the past, people had a tendency to believe that faith necessarily inhibited a successful response to the demands of modern life. This secular bias has proven false in the United States and elsewhere, for many devout believers of every kind bridge the gap between their faith and contemporary life. Globally, we find people of faith holding top positions in government, medicine, law, and the sciences. But this does not mean that some interpretations of faith do not preclude or retard development.

As with religious reform in all faiths, not just in Islam, a critical question always arises: Will the process of renewal be one of restoration or reformation (not necessarily the Reformation)? All authentic religious life and renewal looks back to the past in order to root itself in the foundational texts and principles. The critical distinction is whether religious renewal and reform are based simply upon an attempt to restore or reimplement the doctrinal formulations and laws of the past or whether the process is one of reinterpreting and reapplying sacred texts to the realities and challenges of new contexts. Classical formulations of doctrine and law in religions, while an important part of the legacy of the past, are time bound. Many remain relevant; others do not. If followed slavishly, that which is classical can become medieval.

The distinction between the Shariah and fiqh is critical to reform. One must distinguish between the Shariah, divinely mandated laws or regulations that are universal, and fiqh (understanding), those laws that are the product not simply of divinely revealed texts but of human interpretations developed in response to specific historical and social contexts. This provides a basis for reform. Often the phrase "Islamic law" is used imprecisely and blurs this distinction, thereby sacralizing the corpus of the fiqh (law) of the past and the *fuqaha'* (legal scholars) themselves. Recently I read comments by Muslims who thought that it was simply sufficient to say that a certain activity was not permissible because Imam Malik or Imam al-Shafi'i did not recognize or approve of it. However great, learned, and important they were, these jurists of the past were not infallible.

The relationship of Islamic law to the state can also be viewed in many ways. Differing societies, in the past and certainly in the present and future, may choose diverse paths. While some Muslims may argue that the state must formally implement the Shariah (Islamic law), others may opt for a state in which no law is contrary to the basic tenets of Islam or in which Islamic law is "one" of the sources of law. There are many possibilities. At the same time, Muslims are challenged today not only to recognize but actually to incorporate an internal pluralism, a generous space, in their religious discourse and behavior as they explore and redefine new ways to interpret and apply their faith to issues of pluralism and citizenship, gender roles and marital relations, and so on. Of course, past precedents can be appropriated in this process. For every person who cites ijtihad and the recognition of different opinions (*ikhtilaf*) in Islam, however, there are others for whom Islamization has also meant a process of "kafirization," condemning any who disagree with their opinion.

[**QUESTION 4**] *What is the future of political Islam? Does the emergence of radical groups undermine the legitimacy of Islamic movements in the Muslim World or enhance their appeal? Will we witness a resurgence in the relevance and influence of groups such as the Jamaat-i Islami and the Ikhwan al-Muslimeen, or will they slowly lose ground to more moderate movements? Will political Islamic movements radicalize or democratize?*

JLE: In its narrow sense, political Islam (which has meant the introduction or more often the imposition of Islamic governments) has been seriously discredited by the failures of the Iranian, Sudanese, and Afghani experiments. In addition, both mainstream and extremist Islamic political movements have been severely limited, contained, or crushed by the power of authoritarian regimes such as those of Egypt and Algeria. Al-Qaeda and other radical groups, while remaining attractive and growing as an extremist option, have also contributed to the discrediting of political Islam (or at least the recognition of its potential dark side) among mainstream Muslims who have either been victims or identified with the victims of terrorism in the Muslim World and in the West.

Although the Jamaat and Ikhwan continue to attract members and supporters, many more movements have emerged globally. Also, the level of leadership and influence of the Jamaat and the Ikhwan is more limited than it was years ago. Competition comes not only from the rise of more militant options but also from younger Islamic alternative groups. In addition, if political systems open up and more political parties are able to form and function, Islamic movements, while remaining an important force, will nevertheless no longer be able to count on those who supported or voted for them because they were the "only game in town." They will no longer be the only alternative available to express opposition or to cast a vote against the government. For the foreseeable future, Islamic political movements will continue to follow the paths of both radicalization and democratization. The political, economic, and social realities of individual countries will determine the path of specific movements. A more open political system will enable the development of mainstream Islamic movements that pursue democratization; more repressive regimes, as in the past, will feed the growth of extremism and terrorism.

[QUESTION 5] *What impact will Islam have on the West and on Islamic-Western relations? Is the future of Islam and Muslims in the West in danger?*

JLE: Muslims have become part of the mosaic of North America. True, they do so in diverse ways. Some follow a more isolationist and/or supercritical approach religiously and politically. Others, the majority, have increasingly opted to be American Muslims, much as there have been Egyptian, Sudanese, or Pakistani Muslims. This does not mean that all mainstream Muslims will assimilate in precisely the same way or to the same degree as other Muslims or, indeed, other ethnic and religious groups before them.

American Muslims have made and continue to make significant contributions in defining and redefining Islam in terms of issues of identity (the relationship of religion to culture), pluralism, tolerance, human rights, and democratization. Their influence and impact is felt not only in North America but also globally. North American Muslims have also become an important bridge between Islam and the West, for they are part and parcel of the West: they are citizens, neighbors, workers.

At the same time, post-9/11, the future of Islam and Muslims in the West faces a danger: Islamophobia. This danger affects issues of citizenship, civil liberties, employment, and other areas of life. Islamophobia is a growing reality/threat in North America and in Europe. Polls, studies, and an event like the United Nations conference on Islamophobia hosted by Kofi Annan in 2004 attest to the growth and dangers of Islamophobia. This situation continues to be fed and compounded by the statements and policies of many neoconservatives and representatives of the militant Christian Right (I distinguish between the militant and the mainstream

Christian Right). These well-meaning but ignorant or uninformed leaders and public personalities are often featured in the media, which seek conflict and confrontation.

Finally, no discussion of this last question as well as the previous ones would be complete without some expression of concern regarding Muslim responses post-9/11. While many Muslims have risen to the occasion, many more have not. The issues facing Muslims in the West and those in predominantly Muslim countries require a substantial self-criticism, reform, and the commitment of human and financial resources—not simply from others but from Muslims themselves. Clearly, many Muslims have responded. But this response has fallen far short of what is necessary in today's environment. Among the key issues that Muslims need to address more effectively are the existence and consequences of exclusivist theologies and their impact on pluralism both within the Muslim community and vis-à-vis non-Muslim communities; the extent to which exclusivist theologies, although not in themselves violent, can easily lead to or be transformed by militants into theologies of hate and violence; the need for a balanced refutation of exclusivist or militant Wahhabi or Salafi theological influences in America; and a critique of the illegitimate, un-Islamic excesses committed by Muslims engaged in otherwise legitimate causes of resistance or liberation in the Middle East and Asia.

A far greater recognition of the dimensions of the problems, issues, and threats to the community is required. In addition, more support is needed to generate the enormous human and financial resources necessary for political mobilization, political action committees and lobbying, think-tanks, education, and the media. The skills of many talented Muslim professionals, especially among the younger generation, need to be channeled into voluntary part-time work on the myriad religious, political, economic, and social issues that exist. Moreover, to be blunt, because of the resources available from outside sources, individuals and organizations are in very serious danger of becoming "professional Muslims" who are more content with competing for resources and self-promotion and thus eager to project the profile favored by the funding sources. This approach undermines the kinds of critical, collegial, and coordinated efforts that are required. Muslims still need to learn more and faster from the experiences and example of other ethnic and religious groups who have successfully influenced the system in all of its realms, from politics and religion to the media and education.

Chapter 4

FREEDOM AND SECURITY
Necessary Conditions for Moderation

GRAHAM E. FULLER

[QUESTION 1] *If moderate Muslims are critical to an American victory in the war on terror, why does the U.S. government frequently take steps that undermine moderate Muslims? In your view, who are these moderate Muslims and what are their beliefs and politics?*

GRAHAM E. FULLER (GEF): Who is a moderate Muslim? That depends on who you ask and what that person's (or government's) agenda is. Moderate is also a quite relative term, understood differently by different people. For our purposes here, let's examine two distinct approaches to this question: an American view and a Middle East view of what characterizes a moderate Muslim.

Most non-Muslims would probably define a moderate Muslim as anyone who believes in democracy, tolerance, a nonviolent approach to politics, and equitable treatment of women at the legal and social levels. Today the American government functionally adds several more criteria: a moderate Muslim is one who does not oppose U.S. strategic and geopolitical ambitions in the world, accepts American interests and preferences within the world order, believes that Islam has no role in politics, and avoids any confrontation—even political—with Israel.

The American approach to the Muslim World contains deep internal contradictions and warring priorities. While the Bush administration's self-proclaimed global ideological goal is democratization and "freedom," the reality is that U.S. demands for security and the war against terror take priority over the democratization agenda every time. Democratization becomes a punishment visited upon American enemies rather than a gift bestowed upon friends. Friendly tyrants take priority over those less cooperative moderate and democratic Muslims who do not acquiesce to the American agenda in the Muslim World.

Within the United States itself, the immense domestic power of hard-line pro-Likud lobbies and the Israel-firsters sets the agenda on virtually all discourse concerning the Muslim World and Israel. This group has generally succeeded in excluding from the public dialogue most Muslim (or even non-Muslim) voices that are at all critical of Israel's policies. This de facto litmus test dramatically raises the threshold for those who might represent an acceptable moderate Muslim interlocutor. The reality is that there is hardly a single prominent figure in the Muslim World who has not at some point voiced anger at Israeli policies against the Palestinians and expressed ambivalence toward armed resistance against the Israeli occupation of Palestinian lands. Thus few Muslim leaders enjoying public legitimacy in the Muslim World can meet this criterion these days in order to gain entry to the United States to participate in policy discussions.

In short, being considered a moderate Muslim involves an unrealistic litmus test regarding views on Israel that functionally excludes the great majority of serious voices representative of genuine Muslim thinkers in the Middle East who are potential interlocutors. There is no reason to believe that this political framework will change in the United States anytime soon.

In my view, a moderate Muslim is one who is open to the idea of evolutionary change through history in the understanding and practice of Islam, one who shuns literalism and selectivism in the understanding of sacred texts. A moderate would reject the idea that any one group or individual has a monopoly on defining Islam and would seek to emphasize common ground with other faiths, rather than accentuate the differences. A moderate would try to seek within Islam the roots of those political and social values that are broadly consonant with most general values of the rest of the contemporary world. A moderate Muslim would not reject the validity of other faiths.

Against the realities of the contemporary Middle East, a moderate Muslim would broadly eschew violence as a means of settling political issues but still might not condemn all aspects of political violence against state authorities who occupy Muslim lands by force—such as Russia in Chechnya, Israel in Palestine, or even American occupation forces in Iraq. Yet even here, in principle a moderate must reject attacks against civilians, women, and children in any struggle for national liberation. Moderates would be open to cooperation with the West and the United States, but not at the expense of their own independence and sovereignty.

[**QUESTION 2**] *Is it possible to imagine that the Turkish Islamists, now under the leadership of visionaries such as Prime Minister Erdogan, are the harbingers of moderate Islam and Islamic democracy?*

GEF: Prime Minister Tayyip Erdogan of Turkey's AKP (Justice and Development Party) is without question a central and vital figure in the global evolution of political Islam. The AKP's experience has great relevance for other Muslim states, despite the differing conditions in each country. Actually, the West has not correctly understood the Turkish "secular" experience in its totality, assuming that the Kemalist approach to the total suppression of Islam in the public space and complete state domination over religion is the model for the whole Muslim World. While Mustafa Kemal Atatürk was the savior of his country and a brilliant reformer by any standard, his party's longtime suppression of Islamic political and social forces led to some schizophrenia within the body politic that only now is beginning to be corrected. This correction is leading to social reconciliation and healing as well as the organic integration of Turkey's Islamists into the political order and governance.

In short, we are witnessing a normalization of the Turkish political order through a process of democratization that is moving toward the expression of the full spectrum of political and ideological thinking within Turkey. This process demonstrates the productive evolution of the Islamists as they gain in realism and understanding of the realities of political life within a pluralist and diverse society with strong secular leanings, especially among the elite.

The AKP, furthermore, rigorously maintains that it is not in fact an "Islamist" party, despite its deep roots in that tradition. It states that it is a conservative democratic party that honors and values the past values of Turkey—including its Islamic traditions, its role in Islamic history, the social values and mores of Muslim believers, and the place for religious education within the country—even while seeking modernity through intensified democratization, the spread of civil liberties, a reduced role for the military in Turkish political life, and membership in the European Union (EU).

While some people in and around the Bush administration are beginning to express concern and dismay that the Erdogan government is drifting away from Turkey's formerly staunch support for American policies in the area, in reality Turkey is coming of age politically. As its prospects for entry into the EU improve, Turkey is more freely expressing a new independence of geopolitical thinking in the region that no longer automatically prioritizes American interests. A more mature and diverse Turkish foreign policy is emerging: it is no longer simply Eurocentric (as it has been since the establishment of the Turkish republic) but acknowledges the country's Balkan, Caucasian, and Middle Eastern and Muslim character as well as its European and Mediterranean roots.

Even more importantly, Turkey's newfound independence from predictable conformity with U.S. interests—a shift supported by a great majority of its population—has gained the attention of Turkey's neighbors and the Arab world. These states had long since written off the "old" Turkey as having turned its back on its Islamic and Ottoman heritages in favor of a constant quest and longing for acceptance within the West. The "new" Turkey, more independent in its foreign policies yet reemphasizing its traditional Muslim culture, is now a source of intense interest among many Arab leaders and may well be able to play an independent role in bringing evolution and moderation to the Islamist politics of the Arab and Muslim worlds.

[QUESTION 3] *Do you think that faith in the promise of ijtihad is justified? Where is reform necessary? What do you understand by the term "Islamic reform"? Can Muslims develop modern, democratic, and prosperous societies without abandoning the wisdom and blessings of revelation?*

GEF: The Muslim World cannot evolve, develop, and prosper through the wholesale adoption of American, Western, or other models of governance. Muslim governance must emerge from the history and traditions of each country. Given the importance of the Islamic tradition, it cannot be ignored in future political and social evolution.

The salience of Islamist parties as the single most powerful force in opposition to the authoritarian status quo across so much of the Muslim World is due to public respect for the values and reform goals that these movements represent. But these movements cannot ride forever on evocation of the past and repetition of slogans about the superiority of Islam as "the way" in politics. Islamists must demonstrate that once they gain some political responsibility they can deliver what they promise through wise and effective policies. If they do not deliver, they will fail as political movements and be supplanted by still newer forces seeking reformist goals, change, and progress—probably this time from the left.

But for Islamist parties to succeed, the reform of Islamic thought is required. Too much contemporary Islamic "thinking" is mired in literalism, narrowness of vision, and intolerance. As key Muslim reformers such as Fazlur Rahman have stated, in looking at the Qur'an and the hadith, Muslims must consider not just the text but the context: What are the broader principles and values underlying the language of the Qur'an on specific issues or the decisions and actions taken by the Prophet? How would those values be understood in a contemporary setting? In this sense, Islam must be a vital and living tradition of complete relevance to life in the contemporary world and not based on earlier commentaries and legislations of a different millennium. But such fresh thinking about Islam requires the necessary political and intellectual freedom to explore new avenues of thought without censorship or censure.

Sadly, at least two great hindrances are blocking renewal and creativity in Islamic thinking today. The first is the absence of intellectual, political, and social freedom within most Islamic societies, except in the West. The second is the violent and sweeping nature of the American "global war on terror," with its high dependency upon military action, accompanied by an avowedly hegemonistic American geopolitical strategy. This strategy is rejected by most of the world, but with particular vehemence and emotion by Muslims. The Muslim World, feeling itself under siege and with its sensitivities heightened by witnessing the struggle of Muslims across the global *ummah,* is not currently operating in a environment conducive to either intellectual openness or liberal and reformist thought. It is simply hunkered down in defensive and survivalist mode. Indeed, the forces of terrorism in the Muslim World must be brought to heel. But that will not happen unless we see a change in hegemonistic U.S. policies, America's explicit embrace of Israeli right-wing policies in the occupied West Bank, and its linkage with fundamentalist Christian attitudes.

[QUESTION 4] *What is the future of political Islam? Does the emergence of radical groups undermine the legitimacy of Islamic movements in the Muslim World or enhance their appeal? Will we witness a resurgence in the relevance and influence of groups such as the Jamaat-i Islami and the Ikhwan al-Muslimeen, or will they slowly lose ground to more moderate movements? Will political Islamic movements radicalize or democratize?*

GEF: As long as conditions in the Muslim World remain radicalized—by terrorism, the sweeping U.S. military response, dictatorship across the region, and a sense of Islam being under siege—only radical groups will flourish. Moderation and liberalization can only flourish in a quieter and freer environment, where radical voices find a limited response.

Over time, however, it may be that the violence on both sides and the radicalism of extreme groups will actually serve to widen the spectrum of choice before the broader Muslim public over the longer run. Intolerant proclamations in the name of Islam are actually forcing Muslims to come to terms with the problem: What do they really want and how do they understand Islam and its interrelationship with the world's non-Muslim forces? This process is now slowly underway, not just at the elite level but at the popular level as well, among Muslims whose lives are directly impacted by the violence around them.

Traditional Islamist movements such as the Jamaat-i Islami and the Ikhwan al-Muslimeen may gain greater relevance as the virtues of a less violent and more moderate political vision become evident. But they will also have to "deliver," or else the public will abandon them. Ironically, liberalizing the Muslim World polity can threaten traditional Islamist groups, because they will lose their "privileged" position as a politically repressed group with a limited voice in government; they will gain influence and the ability to bring about change as they play a new role in politics. At that point, they will have no excuse for not "delivering" and will be held accountable in ways that they cannot be held accountable today.

There is little doubt in my mind that Islamist organizations will be required to move toward greater moderation and pragmatism as they enter the political order—or else they will fail. But such a trend toward moderation and liberalization is not in the cards over the short term, given the entrenchment of authoritarianism and the war and bloodshed that dominates the region today.

[QUESTION 5] *What impact will Islam have on the West and on Islamic-Western relations? Is the future of Islam and Muslims in the West in danger?*

GEF: It is absurd to speak of a general "threat" from Muslim minorities to the West. The West is too old, established, culturally experienced, and enriched to be threatened by Islam or any other culture. On the contrary, as the West gradually absorbs and integrates its Muslims, the

Muslim community will contribute to the richness of Western culture via the influx of Islamic ideas and culture, just as other immigrant cultures have contributed in the past.

Two circumstances, however, must be mentioned in this context. First, obviously terrorist acts by Muslims carried out in the West do threaten all who live in Western societies. These must be contained through intelligence and police action and with the support of Muslim communities, which are even more threatened by such acts. This problem is distinctly manageable.

Second, while such immigrant societies as the United States, Canada, and Australia cannot, almost by definition, be seriously threatened culturally by any kind of immigration, countries that are traditional homelands to specific ethnic groups, traditions, and cultures can be "threatened," that is, diluted and weakened by immigration. For example, the Netherlands represents a richly developed and relatively homogeneous Dutch culture maintained by a small population whose traditional character can, in fact, be threatened by any large immigrant influx—Muslim or otherwise. Such societies will have to cope with the serious challenges that globalization presents to so many countries of the world.

In a similar vein, Islamic culture should not be "threatened" through its presence in the West. Islam itself is an incredibly rich culture that has a long history of absorbing those elements of other cultures and civilizations across the globe that have helped to make Islam what it is today. To the extent that Islam remains a living and resilient culture, it can only profit from interaction with the positive elements of Western culture. (Ironically, such interaction may bolster the social and moral critique of the more problematic Western cultural elements.)

Of course, Muslims in the West, just like other immigrants, will lose the particularities of the homeland cultures, including their traditional expression of Islam. But the broader spirit of Islam that exists above local cultural expression—its more universal features—will survive and evolve. To the extent that Islamic culture does not retain its spirit of resilience, innovation, and creativity, however, it might indeed be eroded by its presence in the dynamic West. Once the violent, confrontational phase of Muslim relations with the West—fueled by Osama bin Ladin and the American neoconservative response—has passed, Muslims should cease to represent any "special" element within Western society, apart from the routine immigration problems that every new wave of immigration generates.

There is a significant danger, however, that individuals who are intellectually lazy and prejudiced both in the Muslim World and in the United States may be in the process of accepting the facile "clash of civilizations" concept as the default explanation for what is a complex, many-tiered, and multidimensional phenomenon of the historical confrontation and coexistence between the Muslim World and the West. Under these conditions, we may find ourselves living a self-fulfilling prophecy. I hope that the realities of the world will overcome such simplistic thinking—but that will not happen while the blood is running.

Chapter 5

MODERATE ISLAM

A Product of American Extremism

ABID ULLAH JAN

[QUESTION I] *If moderate Muslims are critical to an American victory in the war on terror, why does the U.S. government frequently take steps that undermine moderate Muslims? In your view, who are these moderate Muslims and what are their beliefs and politics?*

ABID ULLAH JAN (AUJ): The promotion of "moderate" Muslims is part of an extremist tendency sweeping the United States, unlike the situation in the Muslim World. It is the result of a war between two Americas: the America of ideals (such as equality and justice) and the America of extremism, which has succumbed to self-interest groups and individuals. For the America of ideals, the Tariq Ramadan episode is a dark spot, one among many such episodes in recent times. Periodic episodes of tragedy are the hallmark of the America that has shifted its priorities under the pressure and manipulation of the extremists. These forces use all expedient means to sacrifice the well-being of the United States for self-interest and promotion of the Zionist state.

This extremism entails a morbid dread of Islam. It never regards any Muslim as a moderate unless that individual publicly rejects key parts of the Qur'an and belief in it as "the final manifesto of God," which the extremists consider a "disturbing cornerstone of Islam."[1] Unquestioning support for Israel, along with all other American-approved dictatorships, is the minimum criterion.[2] All other factors are irrelevant.

The fascistic American track record of accepting "moderates" and rejecting "radicals" is clear.[3] The final distinction is not defined by their adherence to Islam but by the assumed threat that they pose to the interests of these extremists. For example, a devout Muslim, fervent in observance of all personal rituals but not participating in political affairs, would be a "moderate," whereas a marginally practicing Muslim with the zeal to voice opposition to the injustice perpetrated by the extremists' America would be classified as a "radical."

In the current political context, moderates are passive like the devout Muslims or active like the extremist "moderates"—the Muslim neomods— who openly promote the extremist agenda by using Islamic interpretations or "Project Ijtihad" as a cover.[4] Hence the distinction is not academic or religious but political.

Two opposing factors prove this point. First, Muslims are clearly commanded to be moderate by default.[5] Moderateness is a prerequisite for all Muslims, not a label of identity for some. Accordingly, Muslims cannot be part-time or partial Muslims (Qur'an 2:208) or reject part of the Qur'an (Qur'an 2:85).[6] Hence such religious labeling is irrelevant. Second, the extremists insist that strong belief in the totality of the Qur'an makes Muslims "Islamists."[7] That is why they believe themselves to be "absolutely at war with the vision of life that is prescribed to all Muslims in the Koran."[8] This means that the standards of "moderateness," as set by the American extremists, are directed at neutralizing a preconceived threat. Under these circumstances, mere claims of being a "moderate" do not make any difference at all, as long as Muslims are presented as a threat, however baseless, to the interests of extremist America.

Similarly, the so-called extremism in the Muslim World is not the result of Muslims' faith. Rather, it is a function of the perpetually colonized and oppressed people, due to the lack of true independence and a central authority to control and productively channel their energies. It is naïve to suggest that a few ill-informed "moderate" individuals or puppet regimes can emulate the abilities of an entire central authority (that is, the Islamic state) and effect progress and positive meaningful change.

[**QUESTION 2**] *Is it possible to imagine that the Turkish Islamists, now under the leadership of visionaries such as Prime Minister Erdogan, are the harbingers of moderate Islam and Islamic democracy?*

AUJ: Although the question frames the central problem in reasonable terms, it thereafter descends into fatal assumptions.

First: perpetuating the "Islam vs. the West" paradigm is the real agenda expressed. Are Bosnia and Albania part of "the West"? What about Palestine, if some view Israel as part of "the West"? Also consider the relocation of around 400 million Muslims from Muslim-majority regions during the twentieth century. Or consider Muslims in the United States, who will soon constitute the world's most educated, influential, and wealthy Muslim population. What, then, is "the West"? Instead, a new paradigm is required.

Second: it is ironic and premature to present the intolerant secular regime in Turkey as a beacon of democracy for Muslims. At best, it is a third-rate imitation of the worst of the so-considered West. Without real independence, identity, and vision, Turkey is begging on its knees to enter Europe. The masses still do not identify with the military regime, and the election of yet another Muslim backslider (Erdogan) provides little hope for comprehensive solutions based on Islam.

Third: the use of the pejorative term "Islamic totalitarianism" ignores secularism, which is an ideology every bit as much as any religion is. Islamic totalitarianism is a convenient contrivance, unlike the all-too-familiar secular totalitarianism of the present. Even a loose model like the one under Ayatollah Khomeini clearly had more popular support than any of the present corporate-run secular totalitarianisms.

The heart of actual totalitarianism lies in a system where humanity is sovereign and decides what is right and wrong according to the interests of a minority that plays a preponderant role in power-mongering. From genocides to unrestrained capitalism, colonial domination is a constant feature of secular democracies. Muslims never built gas chambers, used nuclear weapons, or commanded genocidal sanctions against nations that were already on their knees. Islam does not sanction concentration camps and the systematic massacre of non-Muslims.

Fourth: the current emphasis on the ongoing turmoil in the Muslim World ignores the fact that problems in Muslim-majority countries are correlated with the problems in Muslim-minority countries such as India and with various other regions, such as Africa and South America, that may not even have a Muslim presence of any significance.

The fundamental problem is the continued colonial interference in the internal affairs of these countries and their ongoing exploitation by global financial institutions. Regardless of its religious affiliation, no government can thrive under the burden of structural adjustments and the debts owed to these institutions. Even if an Islamic theo-democracy driven by Muslim "moderates" was imposed on Muslim countries, they would still continue to suffer due to external interference, which deprives them of their right to self-determination. Thus all experiments in government other than Muslim self-rule will remain mere exercises in futility.

The problem within the Muslim World is a two-pronged crisis of knowledge and faith: a general lack of both among the masses and an abandonment of both among the educated elite for materialist aims. Simply put, Muslims are proving themselves to be just as capitalistic as the capitalists. The revered generation of Prophet Muhammad (peace be upon him) and his immediate successors was driven by piety and faith. The great Muslim civilizations of history, even if they were faith-driven, still built flourishing civilizations. Thus the Muslims' primary goal is to develop, establish, and nurture a society driven by faith. The structure of government becomes secondary to this goal. Unfortunately, every major Muslim government has drifted away from this foundation.

An Islamic polity would first need to be able to exist without inheriting any of the shackles of its predecessors. Unless it is born from the faith of the masses and the elite, any attempt to implement any sort of Islamic rule would be an unwelcome imposition on a population that is not ready for it. No legitimate government can be implemented through a top-down approach, and an Islamic state is no exception.

[**QUESTION 3**] *Do you think that faith in the promise of ijtihad is justified? Where is reform necessary? What do you understand by the term "Islamic reform"? Can Muslims develop modern, democratic, and prosperous societies without abandoning the wisdom and blessings of revelation?*

AUJ: Ijtihad refers to the complex deliberations involved in providing an understanding of the methods to practice the Qur'anic worldview in any given society. In the matters of individual life, all people are their own masters and can decide as they wish. In matters concerning collective life, however, ijtihad is a tool used to expand Islamic rules and not a license to promote un-Islamic values and norms by giving them Islamic credentials. For decisions regarding collective life, an individual should be competent enough and have an established scholarly position in society to offer an opinion.

There should be genuine demand for forming an expert opinion, as well as an Islamic authority, to make final decisions and act accordingly. This is not presently the case. None of the governments are Islamic; hence none are able to support such an exercise and implement the results. In the depressing state of affairs in Muslim-majority countries, Muslims need to start from somewhere by establishing Islam's system of social justice before engaging in ijtihad on the various nonissues that American extremists have prioritized for them.

Ijtihad is part of the Muslims' struggle for self-determination, because the first requirement is to study the problem in an enlightened fashion and thus understand it completely. Then ijtihad is initiated to determine the means and method to be adopted. This must precede action and thus must occur before the establishment of social justice (for example, the Prophet [peace be upon him] in Mecca struggling against the Quraysh). Ijtihad on issues that require the existence of a legitimate authority to be implemented makes no sense under present conditions.

Even if we try to put the cart before the horse, we must understand what we often overlook in our *ijtihadi* adventures: all such deliberations must connect with the Islamic tradition. Historically, the great reformists were always scholars of the tradition who conducted thorough and deep studies of the Qur'an and hadith. Unfortunately, today we see a double split, at both ends of the spectrum. At one end, the Muslim scholars of Islamic tradition have by and large reduced themselves to government scholars who issue state-approved verdicts and those who are either in jail or keeping a low profile to avoid being sent to jail. At the other end, outspoken Muslims are divided into Muslim scholars who are trained in secular institutions, ideas, and methods and people such as Irshad Manji. Both groups have little connection with the Muslim masses and Islamic tradition and have not sought to acquire a thorough knowledge of the Qur'an and hadith, the Arabic language, and the details of Islamic jurisprudence.

Of course, we need to see some synthesis. Scholars of Islamic tradition have to update themselves so that they can function in today's world; and scholars of the secular fields need to become experts in the Islamic tradition. Nevertheless, they are not living in a static environment with everything waiting for this synthesis. The movement for establishing Islam's just order will grow and grow. It is only a matter of time before the ummah moves from gaining widespread awareness of self-rule (regardless of the title: Islamic state, *khilafah*) to calling loudly for it, to finally effecting it. Until Muslims are willing to revert to Islam and apply it to their individual and collective lives in its true sense, ijtihad will remain little more than a slogan propagated by individuals unqualified to practice it, who will nevertheless impose their own visions—apologetic, self-serving, or militant—on the populace.

[**QUESTION 4**] *What is the future of political Islam? Does the emergence of radical groups undermine the legitimacy of Islamic movements in the Muslim World or enhance their appeal? Will we witness a resurgence in the relevance and influence of groups such as the Jamaat-i Islami and the Ikhwan al-Muslimeen, or will they slowly lose ground to more moderate movements? Will political Islamic movements radicalize or democratize?*

AUJ: The question assumes that "radicalization" and "democratization" are the only two alternatives. This reflects an absolutist mindset. This absolutism has paved the way for the ongoing occupations and for further aggression. The American extremists have failed to present any evidence in support of their justifications for these adventures. The way in which the victims of the present American concentration camps have been treated, their public humiliation in so widespread a fashion, and the lack of any convictions indicate that the U.S. extremists wish to send a message to the Muslims: Do not expect mercy if you dare to oppose American designs. The gratuitous employment of unrestrained torture further demonstrates and emphasizes this point.

No amount of inhumane treatment can ever stand a chance of preventing the so-called specter of political Islam from arising. Actually, there are two sources of "political Islam": (1) material and political and (2) ideological. These will determine its future. So long as Muslims find themselves living under extended colonial and externally imposed or protected regimes in environments that lack opportunity and provide no sense of justice and security, Islam will be sought out as a cure in the political realm.

Due to the economic exploitation by global institutions, the gross domestic product (GDP) of the Muslim nations continues to remain stagnant. While they still struggle to pay off their debts and must cater to the needs of their rising populations, concerned individuals will continue to question the double standards that they face. For example, they see Kuwait receive billions of dollars worth of reparations for its six-month occupation by Iraq, whereas others could not get a dime for reeling under decades of colonial and other occupations.

For recent generations, the answer came in the forms of nationalism and socialism. While it is expected that some form of socialism will return to combat the unrestrained capitalism that is devouring the globe, Islam itself is currently being sought out to provide answers, if not relief. If the material conditions in these societies improve—it is posited—it is unfortunate yet only to be expected that their desires for a worldly Islamic salvation will proportionally decrease. For the casual onlooker, the cure appears to be jobs and security. At the ideological level, however, the situation is rather different. Regardless of the material conditions of their particular societies, some individuals regard Islam as it is: a complete code of life, a *din,* not just a religion or a set of rituals.

Presently, most of these groups are unable to offer a consistent and comprehensive plan of action. In fact, many of them, like the Jamaat-i Islami and the Ikhwan al-Muslimeen, are spent forces. Their raison d'être has been thoroughly compromised in every arena, given that they have failed in their primary mission. Now they are content with charitable actions and mere jockeying for minor positions on the political periphery. "Moderate" movements will come and go in a similar fashion as tastes change. Democracy (read: capitalism) will be tried in the Muslim World to satisfy the interests of the extremists abroad, and it will prove to be just as ruinous as the ideologies such as socialism, Bathism, and nationalism that preceded it. Those who remain steadfast in their belief and stick to the core sources of Islam—the Qur'an and Sunnah—will eventually shine through. Those who have a thorough understanding and a comprehensively sound agenda will manage to effect the change in the ummah that is needed to reestablish the required Islamic polity.

[**QUESTION 5**] *What impact will Islam have on the West and on Islamic-Western relations? Is the future of Islam and Muslims in the West in danger?*

AUJ: The growth in Muslim numbers is absolutely irrelevant. All that matters is their willingness to strive to live by Islam. Muslims without this will have no significance in the West or in the East, as far as relations and dangers are concerned. As we witness today, the Muslims in the United States are on course to becoming the most educated, wealthy, and politically influential population of Muslims on earth.

The contrary applies elsewhere; the populations of Muslim-majority countries continue to reach unimaginable levels of decay and decline. Their economic drain is only surpassed by their brain drain. Outside the Muslim World, the end of the era of the nation-state is occurring: American political imperialism and cultural hegemony, unrestrained capitalism, and the economic practices of the World Bank and the International Monetary Fund (IMF) are devouring most, if not all, other nations.

The United States is undergoing an unprecedented transition. The Protestant majority has ended. Within a few decades, the white majority will also cease to exist. But these cultural changes are insignificant when compared to the downward turn in the country's domestic politics. The only area in which the United States could once claim global superiority—its system of "checks and balances"—is ending. The second area, its free market, is now being reduced to fewer and fewer players possessing an unbridled and unbalanced international reach.

The greatest tragedy is that capitalism is not only devouring the resources of every corner of the globe but simultaneously consuming its culture, morality, and religion. It is a tragedy that humanity has lost its sense of the Creator; now humanity is losing its sense of itself. The results are obvious: the collapse of the family and the ever-increasing violence across the planet. It is unfortunate that the American extremists are ceaselessly blaming Muslims for these ills. Even the worst Muslim militant did not cause any of these problems. The world will discover these extremists for what they really are: irresponsible, self-serving charlatans.

Apart from annihilation (which has happened historically at least twice to major communities in Europe), there is every prospect that Muslims can continue to grow as a community without being assimilated. In some countries (such as the United States), they might become more isolated and stigmatized. This will serve to make them more aware of their Islamic identity, however, and may also draw in further reverts (those who return to Islam) from the rest of the population who are tired of the extremists' jaundiced agenda.

We have evidence that the almost continual free advertising (even in a derogatory manner) that Islam receives will lead to continued interest in the subject and continued higher exposure of the general population to this "exotic" way of life—resulting in further numbers of reverts and still more who question the extremists' perceived wisdom.

The United States can easily deal with the Muslims' physical confrontation with its perpetrated wars and occupations, due to its superior firepower. This is true only if the United States is willing to commit the necessary atrocities en route (which it appears able and willing to do at present). In the battle of ideas, however, the American extremist ideology has little real answer to the *din* of Islam. If Muslims actually choose to practice the Islam they profess, then everyone will benefit. An Islamic renaissance will neither make nor break the "West." Rather, it will uplift it.

Notes

1. "Publisher's Note" in Irshad Manji's latest book, *The Trouble with Islam*. For example, see the preconditions of the self-appointed standard setters for passing the test of moderation (http://www.danielpipes.org/article/2226). "Moderates" must totally reject parts of the Qur'an, such as rejection of the clear commands about inheritance (Qur'an 4:11–14, 4:33, 4:176), court testimony (Qur'an 2:282), and even *riba* (usury) (Qur'an 2:275, 278–79, 3:130, 4:161, 30:39). As another precondition, "moderates" must agree to "scholarly inquiry into the origins of Islam."

2. Although some people instantly blame Daniel Pipes for being a bigot, he is not. He just speaks openly while others like Thomas Friedman beat around the bush. When it comes to supporting and promoting persons like Manji as moderates, however, there is hardly any difference between them. See Friedman's "Brave, Young and Muslim," *New York Times,* March 3, 2005.

3. The record shows that some "moderate" Muslims are rejected as "reformist apologetic" and others are called "radical." See the remarks by Pipes in "The Rock Star and the Mullah—Debate: Democracy and Islam," a Public Broadcasting Service (PBS) debate between Pipes and Muqtedar Khan (http://www.pbs.org/wnet/wideangle/shows/junoon/debate.html). Even Khaled Abou El Fadl's presence in the United States is not appreciated (Daniel Pipes, "Stealth Islamist: Khaled Abou El Fadl," *Middle East Quarterly* [Spring 2004]: http://www.danielpipes.org/article/1841). Kamran Bokhari calls himself a "moderate." See Bokhari's "Is Democracy Kufr?" and "What Is Moderate Islam & Who Are Moderate Muslims?" (December and March 2004 issues of *Q-News*). Yet he is labeled a "radical" and is not spared (see Daniel Pipes, "The U.S. Institute of Peace Stumbles," *New York Sun,* March 23, 2004: http://www.danielpipes.org/article/1659). In contrast, Irshad Manji is presented as a "practicing Muslim" and promoted by Pipes and Friedman and others.

4. See http://www.muslim-refusenik.com/.

5. Being a Muslim, one has to be moderate. See http://www.icssa.org/moderate.html for details. Also see *Sahih Bokhari,* vol. 3, book 40, Hadith 550; vol. 4, book 55, Hadith 629; vol. 7, book 70, Hadith 577; vol. 8, book 76, Hadith 470, 471, and 474; and *Sahih Muslim,* book 32, Hadith 6243. Accordingly, moderate Muslims by default would devote their lives to the service of their Creator above all other devotions; invite others to develop such a relationship with their Creator; stand up against all prohibitions against this relationship (including criticism of any unjust policy of any government); and demand political, social, and economic reforms in the light of revealed wisdom and removal of any sort of injustice. So, based on that simple definition, what is the difference between a moderate Muslim by default and an idealistic American?

6. The Qur'an (5:13–14) condemns those who accept the revealed books in parts.

7. Ibid.

8. Sam Harris, "Mired in a Religious War," *Washington Times,* December 2, 2004 (http://www.washtimes.com/op-ed/20041201-090801-2582r.htm).

Chapter 6

ISLAMIC DEMOCRACY AND MODERATE MUSLIMS
The Straight Path Runs through the Middle

M. A. MUQTEDAR KHAN

[QUESTION I] *If moderate Muslims are critical to an American victory in the war on terror, why does the U.S. government frequently take steps that undermine moderate Muslims? In your view, who are these moderate Muslims and what are their beliefs and politics?*

M. A. MUQTEDAR KHAN (MAMK): The term "moderate Muslims/Islam" is becoming highly contested. What do we really mean when we brand someone as a moderate Muslim? Indeed, the more interesting question is what does the word mean to outsiders looking into Islam and to Muslims looking out from within Islam? As one who identifies himself strongly with the idea of a liberal Islam and also advocates moderation in the manifestation and expression of Islamic politics, I believe it is important that we flesh out this "religio-political identity." Today identity is politicized, and identity construction and sustenance has become a major political goal. In this era when who we are determines what we do politically, it is imperative that we clarify the "we" in politics.

The American media often use "moderate Muslims" to indicate Muslims who are either pro-Western in their politics or self-critical in their discourse. Therefore, both President Hamid Karzai of Afghanistan and Professor Tariq Ramadan wear the label with felicity: the former for his politics, the latter for his ideas. Ramadan, who is critical of intolerance in Muslim communities and is a strong advocate of the Europeanness of European Muslims as well as a major voice in the articulation of the emerging form of European Islam, in many ways embodies both categories. He is pro-Western as well as self-critical. In spite of his impeccable credentials as a prominent moderate Muslim, the U.S. government recently revoked his work visa, citing vague reasons of national security.

This decision sends the dubious message that when the criteria of pro-Westernism/pro-Americanism and self-critical politics clash, the government chooses the former and civil society chooses the latter. Ramadan's visa was canceled because, in the government's perception, he could pose a national security risk. Interestingly, this evoked an uproar of discontent from civil society and strong voices condemning this decision by the government, particularly within the American academic community.

In general, Muslims do not like using the term "moderate," "progressive," or "liberal" Muslim, for they understand it to indicate an individual who has sold out politically to the "other" side. Others insist that no such thing as moderate or radical Islam exists; there is "only one Islam"—the true Islam—and all other expressions are falsehoods espoused by the *munafiqeen* (hypocrites) or the *murtaddun* (apostates). Of course, the unstated politics behind this dogmatic position is "My interpretation of Islam is obviously the true Islam, and all those who diverge from my position are risking their faith."

In some internal intellectual debates, "moderate Muslim" is used pejoratively to indicate a Muslim who is more secular and less Islamic than the norm, which varies across communities. In the United States, a moderate Muslim is one who peddles a softer form of Islam (the Islam of John Esposito and Karen Armstrong), is willing to coexist peacefully with peoples of other faiths, and is comfortable with democracy and the separation of politics and religion.

Both Western media and Muslims do a disservice by branding some Muslims as moderate solely on the basis of their politics. In general, these people should be understood as self-serving opportunists. In this debate, Esposito refers to them as professional Muslims. That leaves intellectual positions as the criteria for determining who is a moderate Muslim—and especially in comparison to whom, since "moderate" is a relative term. I see moderate Muslims as reflective, self-critical, and pro-democracy and human rights and as closet secularists. Their secularism is American in nature; that is, they believe in the separation of church and state, but not like the French, who prefer to exile religion from the public sphere. But who are moderate Muslims different from and how?

I believe that moderate Muslims are different from militant Muslims, even though both of them advocate the establishment of societies whose organizing principle is Islam. The difference between moderate and militant Muslims lies in their methodological orientation and in the primordial normative preferences that shape their interpretation of Islam. For moderate Muslims, ijtihad is the method of choice for sociopolitical change and military jihad the last option. For militant Muslims, military jihad is the first option and ijtihad is not an option at all.

Ijtihad, narrowly understood, is a juristic tool that allows independent reasoning to articulate Islamic law on issues where textual sources are silent. The unstated assumption is that reason must be silent when the texts have spoken. But, increasingly, moderate Muslim intellectuals see ijtihad as the spirit of Islamic thought that is necessary for the vitality of Islamic ideas. Without ijtihad, Islamic thought and Islamic civilization fall into decay.

For moderate Muslims, ijtihad is a way of life that simultaneously allows Islam to reign supreme in the heart and allows the mind to experience the unfettered freedom of thought. Moderate Muslims are therefore those who cherish freedom of thought while recognizing the existential necessity of faith. They aspire to change, but through the power of mind and not by planting mines.

Moderate Muslims desire a society—a city of virtue—that will treat all people with dignity and respect (Qur'an 17:70). There will be no room for political or normative intimidation (Qur'an 2:256). Individuals will aspire to live an ethical life, for they will recognize its desirability. Communities will compete in doing good, and polities will seek to encourage good and forbid evil (Qur'an 5:48 and 3:110). Moderate Muslims believe that internalizing Islam's message can bring about the social transformation necessary for establishing the virtuous city. The only arena in which moderate Muslims permit excess is in idealism. The Qur'an advocates moderation (2:143) and extols the virtues of the straight path (1:1–7). For moderate Muslims, the middle ground, the common humanity of all, is the straightest path.

[**QUESTION 2**] *Is it possible to imagine that the Turkish Islamists, now under the leadership of visionaries such as Prime Minister Erdogan, are the harbingers of moderate Islam and Islamic democracy?*

MAMK: It has been over half a century since the Muslim World freed itself from European colonialism. In this period, however, the Muslim World has failed to produce a viable and appreciable model of self-governance. The frequent shifts in regime type—as in Pakistan, which oscillates between democracy and dictatorship—are indicative of the unsettled nature of political structures in the Muslim World. Only nations with tyrannical dictatorships and monarchies have enjoyed some degree of political stability, but without significant economic or human development.

Disenchantment in the Muslim World today remains at such high levels that it is the most volatile region on the planet. Today the Muslim World boasts a diversity of regime types: dictatorships and sham democracies in Egypt, Sudan, and Tunisia; secular democracy in Turkey; monarchies in the Gulf; pluralist democracies in Bangladesh and Malaysia; and an Islamic state in Iran (a sort of theo-democracy). Iran, however, lacks the stability and vitality now normally expected of thriving democracies in the First World as well as former Third World countries (like the United States, the United Kingdom, and India).

There is a growing consensus among experts and the masses alike that democratization will reduce many of the Muslim World's problems. Recent surveys have indicated that over 80 percent of Muslims would like to see their countries democratize. Except for a rather radical brand of Islamists who reject every form of democracy in favor of a nebulous notion of an Islamic state/caliphate, most Islamists are now converging with secularists and moderate Muslims on the desirability of democracy. The only question that really needs to be settled is the role of Islam in the Muslim public sphere. Most Islamists will break from this emerging ijma' (consensus) if the preferred model of democracy is secular.

The secularists and moderates are nervous about accepting the Shariah as a prominent basis for Islamic democracy, fearing the implementation of medieval articulations of Islamic criminal codes. The issue of the role of women and the status of religious minorities is also a concern if the polity is completely theocratic, as in Iran. But Muslims, regardless of their political persuasion, believe that Islam has a lot of good to offer and that it must play a role in the public sphere. This global debate among Muslims was played out in the discussions of interim laws for Iraq and Afghanistan as they democratize under the jurisdiction of the American occupation forces.

So far the polities of the Muslim World have not reached a consensus on the role of Islam and things Islamic (laws, clerics, scholars). While the masses in the Islamic Republic of Iran are clamoring for more freedom and political and cultural liberalization, we are also witnessing extremists demanding greater Islamization in another Islamic state: Saudi Arabia. Islamists continue to demand a broader application of the Shariah in places like Turkey and Pakistan; but in those same countries we also see significant opposition to Islamists from secular authoritarian regimes that enjoy sufficient support to prevent popular Islamic revolutions.

The idea of an Islamic democracy that recognizes religious and political freedoms but also acknowledges that Islam has a central role to play in the public sphere and in Muslim individual and collective identity is the best middle path between secular authoritarianism and Islamic fundamentalism. I am not convinced that Turkey is the model for Muslim societies.

While democratic, Turkey is fundamentalist in its advocacy of secularism. In addition, its human rights record could be much better. Nevertheless, Prime Minister Erdogan, who was recently recognized as the European personality of the year (2004), and his cohort of moderate Muslims are great role models for the Muslim World. They are demonstrating how Muslims can navigate this tension between secular authoritarianism and religious fundamentalism.

Turkish leaders have shown that they can improve relations with the West and gain respect in the Muslim World without resorting to either violence or extremism. Prime Minister Erdogan has also shown how one can be a democrat without give up one's Islamic identity or values.

[**QUESTION 3**] *Do you think that faith in the promise of ijtihad is justified? Where is reform necessary? What do you understand by the term "Islamic reform"? Can Muslims develop modern, democratic, and prosperous societies without abandoning the wisdom and blessings of revelation?*

MAMK: One of the most popular explanations for the decline of the great Islamic civilization of the classical era is the idea that the doors of ijtihad were closed, which resulted in the intellectual stultification of an entire civilization. Out of this stultification came the modern Muslim World—a weak and deplorable shadow of its former self. This claim is based on the belief that ijtihad is a vital process of intellectual rejuvenation. Unfortunately, this is not entirely true.

The Muslim World has two conceptions of ijtihad. One is a very narrow juristic notion that essentially states that ijtihad is a process of juristic reasoning employed to determine the permissibility of some action according to the Shariah when primary sources (the Qur'an and Sunnah) are silent and earlier scholars did not rule on the matter. For those who hold this view of ijtihad, who can do ijtihad is often more important than the need for ijtihad. This narrow definition limits who can do ijtihad and what issues can be addressed. In reality, this view is designed to stifle independent thought among Muslims and to restrict the right to understand and explain Islam only to Muslim jurists. It is also opposed to reason, because it essentially says that reason shall be employed only when the texts are silent and no medieval scholar addressed the issue. Reason, according to this viewpoint, is the last resort to understand the will of God. For those who hold this narrow view, opening the doors of ijtihad would make no difference, because their very conception of it is impoverished and limited.

The second view, often employed by nonjurists and particularly by those who advocate some form of Islamic modernism and Islamic liberalism, envisions ijtihad more broadly. For modernist Muslims—and I believe that Islamic modernism deeply influences all moderate Muslim thinking—ijtihad is about freedom of thought, rational thinking, and the quest for truth through multiple epistemologies: science, rationalism, human experience, critical thinking, and so forth. When modernist Muslims claim that the door of ijtihad was closed, they are lamenting the loss of the spirit of science and inquiry that was so spectacularly demonstrated by classical Islamic civilization at its peak. We are nostalgic for Ibn Sina and Ibn Rushd, for al-Farabi, al-Biruni, and al-Haytham. They were scientists and philosophers; some were also jurists. Whatever it is called—some of us call it ijtihad (my personal website is www.ijtihad.org)—this spirit of inquiry and desire for all forms of knowledge, not just religious and juristic, needs to be revived to revitalize and restore Islamic civilization.

As long as the majority of Muslims equate Islam with Shariah and Islamic scholarship with fiqh (jurisprudence), limit real knowledge to only juristic knowledge of Islam, and view ijtihad as a limited jurisprudential tool, closed minds will never open. Islamic modernists have been trying since the time of Sir Syed Ahmad Khan to instill an understanding of the value of knowledge and appreciation for science and philosophical inquiry. Yet there is no research institution worthy of recognition in the entire Muslim World. Muslims must all go back and read Ibn Rushd and see how he bridged science and religion in order to understand that Islam has nothing to fear from reason; they must also open their hearts and minds to rational thought. This is the goal and the philosophy that Ibn Khaldun would have called the "engine of civilization." Modernist Muslims subscribe to and advocate this spirit of Islam, whether it is called ijtihad or *ruh al-'umran* (the soul of civilization).

Islamic reformation can be understood in two different ways. It can mean the reform of society (*islah*) to bring it closer to Islamic norms and values. Most Islamic and Islamist reformers are pursuing this type of reform. The other reform strategy is to question the extant understanding of Islam and seek to articulate a reformed understanding of it. This is where Islamic modernists and rationalists have always plied their trade. Here ijtihad is employed as an instrument to critique traditional understanding and rearticulate a more compassionate, more modern, and perhaps even liberal understanding. One area in which Islamic reformist thinking is taking place is the rethinking of the relationship between democracy and Islam.

Both of these approaches hold Islam's divine sources, especially the Qur'an, to be sacred and do not question their ultimate authority, although they may dispute human interpretations of these sources. Moderate and modernist Muslim thinkers also ensure that the secondary source—the Prophetic tradition—is treated as a secondary source and not as another form of revelation. Some people may even seek to reform, reject, or recast revelation; however, they face the danger of trivializing revelation and essentially losing the very essence of faith. These reformers will probably have no impact whatsoever on the Muslim society, regardless of their success with non-Muslim audiences.

In my opinion, Muslims can modernize without fully de-Islamizing or doing away with tradition. India and Japan have shown that societies can modernize without losing their traditional cultures. Muslim societies today have to distinguish between what is Islam and what is culture, retain their Islamic essence, and reform dysfunctional cultural habits that hinder development, progress, equality, and prosperity. Without holding fast to revelation, Muslims will lose their connection with the divine, which would render life meaningless and without purpose. Our challenge today is to benefit from democracy, modernity, and globalization without cutting the umbilical cord to the heavens. I believe that we can do it. American Muslims are demonstrating this in their lives.

[**QUESTION 4**] *What is the future of political Islam? Does the emergence of radical groups undermine the legitimacy of Islamic movements in the Muslim World or enhance their appeal? Will we witness a resurgence in the relevance and influence of groups such as the Jamaat-i Islami and the Ikhwan al-Muslimeen, or will they slowly lose ground to more moderate movements? Will political Islamic movements radicalize or democratize?*

MAMK: There is no doubt that the Muslim World is experiencing great turmoil and instability and that many things will change, including the governing structures of most Muslim countries, before they stabilize. The September 11 attacks on the United States and Washington's response, particularly its invasion of Iraq, are triggering changes in society as well as in the balance of power within various groups in Muslim societies.

A significant growth in the jihadi phenomenon is being fueled by an unprecedented anger and hatred toward the United States. Initially, the jihadis limited their scope of operations to Afghanistan, Saudi Arabia, Africa, Chechnya, and Kashmir. But since the U.S. invasion of Iraq, they have been operating in Europe (Spain and Turkey), Indonesia, North Africa (the Maghreb), Iraq, and Qatar. In addition, they have stepped up the intensity of their operations in Saudi Arabia. While a majority of Muslims are appalled at their tactics, a significant minority support them and will join them in their endeavors. The jihadis have stolen the thunder from the regular political Islamists, who now look moderate and respectable compared to them and have even become acceptable to Washington. From Qazi Hussain Ahmad in Pakistan to Ayatollah Sistani in Iraq, the United States is willing to work with Islamists whenever and wherever it can. There is a distinct possibility that the jihadi phenomenon will grow and keep the Muslim World embroiled in internal and external violence and war for decades to come.

The jihadis have thus moved from the fringe of the Islamist sector to the center of global politics. Other Islamists now have very few options. They can either adjust to their new position as moderates (which would reduce their appeal to their constituency, who could increasingly abandon them to follow the jihadis) or adopt more radical postures in order to remain important. A third option, perhaps the wisest one, would be for the Islamists to join the demand-for-democracy bandwagon across the Muslim World and enjoy the fruits of democracy. The price that they would have to pay for this is the dilution of their Islamist agenda; in other words, they would need to become reconciled to advocating Islamism in proportion to what the traffic can bear.

While the jihadis are ascendant, so are Muslim democrats. The pressure for democratization being applied by Washington has emboldened the pro-democracy sector in the Muslim World, particularly in the Arab Middle East. The momentum for democracy had been gradually developing across the region but had remained more or less under the radar. But now, with elections in Iraq, Palestine, and Saudi Arabia, the mood is much more in favor of democracy. Initially, the Islamists stand to gain from the elections, because they are the best-organized political parties in the Arab world. But it is quite likely that their initial gains will soon decrease if they seek to institutionalize their political rhetoric of opposition to globalization and to the West.

Political Islam's future depends on the prospects for democracy in the Arab world. With democracy comes power but also accountability in real terms for the Islamists. So far all they have done is launch discourses. Once in power, they will have to deliver—and whether they can do so remains to be seen. If they follow the example of the Islamists in Turkey and focus on effective governance and eschew ideological battles at home and abroad, then they will thrive. Otherwise they may become marginalized.

Another important element that will influence the Islamists' future is their relationship with the jihadis. Will they co-opt them, oppose them (indeed, fight them if Islamists come to power), or ignore them? If the Islamists come to power, then they will become the jihadis' target and, in turn, will have to go after the jihadis. So far the Islamists have played both sides. While they have asserted to the rest of the world that Islam does not advocate terrorism, within Muslim discussions they have made excuses for jihadis in Iraq, and some are even partial to Bin Laden. We must remember, however, that the jihadis themselves despise the Islamists. Ayman al-Zawahiri's *al-Hisad al-Murr* (The Bitter Harvest) was a diatribe against Ikhwan al-Muslimeen.

[QUESTION 5] *What impact will Islam have on the West and on Islamic-Western relations? Is the future of Islam and Muslims in the West in danger?*

MAMK: Islam has already had a huge impact on the modern West. Some Muslim philosophers believe that the modern West is the imagination of Ibn Rushd. Islamic ideas have influenced all the fundamental assumptions of modernity. But the contemporary impact of Islam on the West is coming more from demography than from philosophy. Islam is the fastest-growing religion in the West and has become the second largest in Europe, North America, and Australia. In England even the House of Lords has Muslims; in Canada there is an active process of implementing Shariah laws (voluntarily); and Islam continues to thrive in the United States in spite of severe setbacks in the wake of 9/11.

The presence of a large number of Muslims who are determined to resist assimilation poses several challenges to the West. First, it puts pressure on the West to live up to its claims that it is a society that believes in religious tolerance, pluralism, and democracy. The United States has for a long time remained a deeply Christian nation while claiming that it is a secular and pluralist society. The arrival of Muslims is testing this. The Patriot Act, which profiles Muslims; the rise of Christian evangelism, whose rhetoric demonizes Islam; a new foreign policy that is determined to use force to crush and transform the Muslim World; and the scandals of torture and unconscionable conduct at Abu Ghraib and Guantanamo Bay are all signs that the United States has difficulty in living up to its own values when interacting with Muslims. Perhaps democracy was always fragile in the West, and the advent of Muslims only exposed it. But with the emergence of both American and European Muslim identities, the West will also discover that it has allies within its Muslim populations who are equally determined that Western claims to democracy and freedom of religion will be substantiated in reality and in policy.

The Muslim presence in the West has the potential to improve Muslim-Christian and Muslim-Jewish relations through the various interfaith dialogues that are taking place today. Interfaith meetings and Muslims lecturing in churches and synagogues are now regular events in Europe and in North America. These reflect genuine theological developments and also mutual recognition and appreciation that could eventually have a global impact.

As the Muslims' influence increases, they will have an impact on public policy, including the foreign policies of Western nations. Many commentators believe, as the question suggests, that one important reason for the growing unease in the transatlantic alliance is a result of European governments' becoming more responsive to their Muslim populations. American Muslim influence on U.S. policy is neutralized by the more powerful and well-entrenched pro-Israeli lobby, which has strong constituencies in the American Jewish and Christian Evangelical communities. When the Arab-Israeli conflict is finally resolved, the Jewish-Christian alliance on Israel may well split, to give way to a Muslim-Jewish alliance that will seek to counter and contain the growth of Christian evangelism in the United States and the threat it poses to secularism. The American Muslim influence on U.S. foreign policy will thereby greatly increase and have a positive impact on American relations with the Muslim World.

The biggest impediment to the growing influence of Islam and Muslims in the West is the growth of Islamophobia as a result of the aftermath of the September 11 attacks. Some commentators fear that the very future of Islam in the West is at stake, as Islamophobia rises to unprecedented levels. Western nations are compromising their own values—the very values that enable Islam to thrive—in order to marginalize Muslims and reduce their ability to influence domestic and global politics.

Islamophobia in the West depends on two key factors: the rise of anti-Americanism and jihadism in the Muslim World, which demonizes the West as well as the Christian and Jewish faiths, and the rise of evangelical Christianity in the United States, which demonizes Islam and sees it as a barrier to its own global expansion and domination. If the jihadis continue to attack Western targets and employ terrorism as their main weapon, then Islamophobia will thrive in the West and stifle the growth of Islam there. If Christian evangelism continues to strengthen the Christian voting block, it will subvert the very foundations of U.S. democracy and put the prosperity and well-being of Muslims and all other religious minorities at grave risk. The Christian Right is a grave and gathering danger to Islam and democracy, to use the vocabulary of President Bush.

In this political environment, moderate American Muslims have a special role to play. They are uniquely positioned: unlike any other party, they take pride in belonging to both civilizations. They are proud of their Islamic heritage and values and are deeply in tune with their Americanness. For them, the Muslim World and the United States are like two parents between whom they cannot countenance any strife. American Muslims look backward and forward. They are connected here and there, and from this unique position they must advance a balanced discourse of Islam and of the West. They must act not only as Islam's ambassadors to the West but also as American ambassadors to the Muslim World. American Muslims have to be both critical and self-critical. They have to revisit theology and also partake in politics.

In this current situation, moderate American Muslims are the middle ground through whom the straight path passes.

{ III }

THE REBUTTALS

Chapter 7

BLAMING THE UNITED STATES, ISRAEL, OR CAPITALISM IS NOT THE SOLUTION

ARIEL COHEN

THE MAJORITY OF PARTICIPANTS (Cohen, Esposito, Fuller, and Khan) share the concern that militant and violent adherents of radical political Islam—"jihadis," for lack of a better term—may radicalize the West's attitude not only toward Western Muslims but, more importantly, toward Islam as a whole. Indeed the continuation of terrorism against Western interests will likely result in either an American or a combined Western future political and military response. The result of either action may be more involvement by the United States in the Greater Middle East, though, ironically, we need to remember that it is the radicals who would in fact prefer that the United States pull out of the region.

Terrorism is also the cause of what some authors refer to as "Islamophobia," a phenomenon that remains quite rare despite the events of 9/11. Though a greater number of anti-Jewish incidents than anti-Islamic incidents were reported in the United States in 2004, we could assume that the jihadis would prefer to see anti-Muslim incidents carried out by Americans to increase. Aberrant American actions, especially if they are blown out of proportion by the media in the United States and abroad, might radicalize Muslims and cause the jihadis' ranks to swell.

Cohen, Esposito, Fuller, and Khan also agree upon the necessity for a broader interpretation of the meaning of ijtihad as a tool for modernization of the Muslim World. Jan, however, formulates a traditionalist/fundamentalist position regarding ijtihad, viewing it as a tool that only the ulama can wield. He believes that mass and elite indoctrination along the lines of traditional orthodox Islam will bring about the establishment of a pan-Islamic state like a khilafah. Most other participants disagree with such a prognosis.

Unfortunately, Esposito, Fuller, and Jan launch quite vitriolic and misplaced attacks against the supporters of Israel. They refer to them by different names: "pro-Likud lobbies," "extremists," or supporters of the "Zionist state." The topic of Arab-Israeli relations has little to do with the questions at hand: moderate Islam vs. radical Islam and the future of political Islam. If Israel never existed, the extremists would identify other issues to fight about. Israel-bashers fall prey to—or are indeed intentional mouthpieces for—a conspiracy theory of the worst kind: an ideological canard that the United States, or even the world, is run by the Jews. These modern simulacra certainly resemble something out of the Protocols of the Elders of Zion, a tsarist secret service (Okhrana) piece of anti-Semitic disinformation, or the vitriolic rhetoric of *Der Stürmer,* the Nazi propaganda weekly rag. Take Jan's 2003 response ("The Façade of Israel's Reality," http://www.mediamonitors.net/abidullahjan33.html) to Husain Haqqani's article in the *Nation:*

> Wrapped in nicely worded prescriptions for the well-being of Pakistan, there are well-studded gems for pleasing [the] master of our destiny, the Zionists in the U.S.
>
> Realising Zionist power, the chief opportunist, General Musharraf, took the lead through covert promises of recognising Israel during his visit to the U.S. The intellectual mercenaries are now trying to catch up with some confused mixture of rejecting Musharraf and accepting Israel.

Here you have it all: Pervez Musharraf as a puppet of "Zionist power," "intellectual mercenaries," and American "Zionists" as masters of Jan's destiny as well as Leninist (or Nazi) invective and conspiracy theories—and a failed forecast: in the end, Pakistan did not recognize the Jewish state. Badmouthing the Likud is particularly bizarre, if not hypocritical, for it has not championed Greater Israel for over two decades. In recent years its leader, Ariel Sharon, has become a supporter of retreat from Judea, Samaria, and Gaza. Currently he advocates a complete pullout from Gaza with no Palestinian concessions, not even a ceasefire, in return. The Likud that Sharon leads has also become a proponent of an independent Palestinian state, something that Israel-bashers choose to ignore. They call the existence of an "Israeli state in Palestine" just as illegitimate as the Russian occupation in Chechnya or the American occupation in Iraq. Fuller, for example, does not even bother to distinguish between Israel's 1949 and 1967 cease-fire lines, effectively denying Jews the right to their own state—a supreme act of Jew-hatred.

At no point do Esposito, Fuller, and Jan raise the desirability of the Arab-Israeli peace settlement. They do not condemn the brainwashing for violence by Hamas and Hizbollah and, for that matter, remain effectively mum regarding the necessity to end the jihadis' anti-American propaganda in Salafi/Wahhabi mosques in the Middle East, Europe, and the United States. The only mention of the jihadi vitriol is wrapped in polite words about "exclusivist theologies," which require an open and painful debate within the Islamic world. Those governments and foundations that fund such activities should cease and desist from doing so.

Allegations that the American right-wing media define the image of Muslims in this country are without intellectual merit. American political discourse and the media are much broader than the *National Review* or the *New York Post*. In today's media market, participants in this debate are often the "talking heads" who provide commentary on "untainted" channels. Pillars of the American liberal media, such as the Cable News Network (CNN), Public Broadcasting System (PBS), *New Yorker, New York Times,* and *Los Angeles Times,* for example, aired and published an excellent journalistic investigation of radical Islamist education/propaganda. The notion that the image of Muslims in the American media is controlled by Jews, neoconservatives, and the Christian Right is bogus. American media are pluralistic in terms of ownership and politics. Unlike the situation in many countries around the globe, there is a true plurality of opinion in the American print and electronic media, including the Internet.

Generally speaking, blaming the United States, Israel, or even capitalism for the sorry state of the Muslim World today (especially in the areas of education and economics), as Jan and others excel in doing, will not contribute to finding workable solutions for that vast expanse from Morocco to Indonesia. In fact Sudan and Afghanistan did worse, not better, under Islamist leadership. Nor does it help to compare or equate Bin Laden's murderous crimes with a morally justified American military response.

It is also a falsehood to say that the United States does not deal with Muslim regimes that disagree with it or that engage in political confrontation with Israel. The United States deals extensively with the Kingdom of Saudi Arabia, an opponent of the war in Iraq and a known financier of the Palestinian Authority and Hamas. The United States also deals on a daily basis with Turkey, Egypt, Indonesia, Bangladesh, and other Muslim countries. And the United States promoted and continues to promote democracy vis-à-vis rulers who at one time were its staunch allies, including Ferdinand Marcos of the Philippines, Edward Shevardnadze of Georgia, and Leonid Kuchma of Ukraine. Moreover, the United States supported democratic forces in Ukraine to the detriment of its Iraq policy: Victor Yushchenko, the newly elected president of Ukraine, promised to pull the 1,600-strong Ukrainian contingent out of Iraq by the end of 2005.

The discussion of the future viability of political Islam, including its more radical components, in the debate is satisfactory. Muqtedar Khan in particular emphasizes his vision of moderate Islam, bridging the two civilizations of Islam and the West. What is lacking so far is a clearer and sharper focus on the probable consequences of those governmental policies that the radicals advocate and may implement if they should assume power. For example, would the stagnant economies of the Muslim World, a reality that Jan mistakenly attributes to "colonialism," blossom under radical Islam? Certainly not, if radicals continue to reject capitalism and foreign investment. Jan, blinded by his hatred toward the International Monetary Fund (IMF) and the World Bank's policies (which are far from perfect), forgets that Muslim countries with huge inflows of capital from oil exports have failed to create a transparent system of wealth distribution. At the same time he conveniently ignores a number of formerly impoverished countries, especially in East Asia but also in Latin America and Eastern Europe, that have managed to demonstrate very impressive growth rates in the fifty years since decolonization—without introducing Shariah law and by following the same capitalist model that he rejects.

Furthermore, Jan believes that the establishment of a Shariah-based superstate will manage to resolve some of the most acute contradictions of today's mainstream Islam: the inferior status and rights of women and the failure of secular education. On the contrary, the emergence of a khilafah will only worsen the situation by using the powers of the state to marginalize women, thereby empowering the most misogynistic elements across Muslim societies.

Jan chose as a model a premodern Islamic state. Most would describe this model as more ideological than Soviet communism, a failed ideology that tried to control all aspects of life—just as Jan suggests for his Islamic utopia. There, as Jan prescribes, the "priest class," steeped in Marxist-Leninist tenets of dialectical materialism and "scientific communism," controlled all facets of society, including science, technology, and administration, through the Communist Party apparatus. Scientists and technocrats were exhorted to "learn" Marxism-Leninism and submit themselves to the diktats of the party.

To get a better picture, it will suffice to read *1984* by George Orwell and books by Alexander Solzhenitsyn, Arthur Koestler, and any of the dissident Soviet and Eastern European writers. What Jan is advocating is nothing less than an Islamist dictatorship that will find itself in a perennial struggle with the rest of the world, not just the United States. If such an entity is created and obtains nuclear weapons (perhaps from the current Pakistani, Iranian, or North Korean arsenals), the world may face nuclear annihilation. To avoid such a scenario, it is important for moderate Muslims, as Muqtedar Khan so eloquently describes, to raise their heads.

It is vital for the future of Islam that tolerant pluralistic and nonviolent paths be elaborated and that they win the competition against retrogrades and hatemongers. They will lead to more democracy, participation, and transparency in Muslim societies and are likely to ameliorate the plight of women and minorities. Moderate leaderships are more likely to engender economic development, which leads to prosperity and rising living standards, including higher rates of charity—an important virtue in all three monotheistic religions.

It is imperative for the United States and the West to recognize, support, and embrace those moderate voices, while remaining vigilant against the threats of radicalism, militancy, and terrorism.

Chapter 8

THE CLASH OF IGNORANCES

The War on Terror Must Not
Compromise Muslim Rights

JOHN L. ESPOSITO

THE RESPONSES OF MY COLLEAGUES provide a good representation of the extraordinarily diverse views of Islam, Muslims, and Muslim politics that exist today.

Like it or not, we are stuck with the phrase "moderate Muslim." Yet as I read our comments I keep thinking that for too many, non-Muslims and Muslims alike, moderate means someone "like us." Thus moderate is equated with progressive or liberal Muslims but excludes conservatives or traditionalists. Ariel Cohen, in his identification of several moderate Muslims, mentions Amina Wadud's leading of a mixed-gender Friday prayer. This underscores the problem with the term "moderate," especially when it is juxtaposed with "extremist." If a woman leading an official prayer service was a criterion for being moderate, then many Christian and Jewish groups, denominations, and their leaders (for example, Pope John Paul II) would fail the test and not be moderates. But they certainly would not be extremists either. Should we then add other litmus tests such as positions on birth control, abortion, and gay rights?

If we go down this road, I wonder how Jews and Christians would react to Muslim countries or Muslim experts and political commentators who attempted to set the definition of a moderate Jew or a moderate Catholic, with the implication that all others were extremists. If, as some non-Muslims have done with regard to Islam, Muslims established institutes and think-tanks to define, monitor, or implement their notions of a moderate Jew or moderate Christian, how long would it be before they would be accused of being anti-Semitic or anti-Catholic? Would we define a moderate Jew vs. an extremist Jew as one who rejects scriptural justification for claims to Israel; rejects the logic and creation of settlements by religiously motivated Jews; possesses an enlightened understanding of the origins of Judaism and of the Hebrew scriptures; rejects all those biblical passages in which God commands acts of violence and warfare; and eschews any mixing of faith with politics in Israel with the support of fundamentalist or religious nationalist groups, schools, or settlements?

A final point regarding moderate Muslims (one raised by Cohen) is related to the Bush administration's handling, or mishandling, of the case of Professor Tariq Ramadan as well as that of Yusuf Islam. Both reinforce the belief that a Muslim who takes issue with any U.S. policy will fail the moderate Muslim test. Ramadan has a long-established record, attested in his writings, media appearances, and public talks internationally. The revocation of his visa, with no official reasons given, drew an international response, including a cross section of scholars, who supported Ramadan's right to hold his positions, whether they agreed with him or not. If the American administration or the French government, which has been extraordinarily aggressive on this issue, has hard or damning evidence against Ramadan, it should provide it.

Ramadan is an internationally recognized scholar, a reformist voice, and a bridge builder, as evidenced in his most recent book, *Western Muslims and the Future of Islam,* as well as his earlier *To Be a European Muslim.* At the same time, he is an independent Muslim voice in both the Muslim community and the international community. Cohen speaks of a case based on "assumptions" regarding Ramadan but then proceeds to provide no hard evidence or documentation for his unsubstantiated accusations. Instead, we are given a series of allegations based on Ramadan's family tree, suspicions, and speculation from media reports, with the major citation coming from the "Militant Islam Monitor" website, which features the militant opinions of Daniel Pipes and Steven Emerson.

Cohen's unsubstantiated charges continue: "The American government allows radical Muslims who support terrorism to operate with impunity in the United States and around the world and does very little to support moderate Muslims, especially in the conflict zones." He offers no evidence. As we look at the thousands of Muslims arrested or detained after 9/11 and the many Islamic charities and institutes raided or closed post-9/11, we must ask: how many have been found guilty of committing or supporting acts of terrorism? The threat of terrorism does exist, as does the presence of radical Muslims in the United States. To charge that government agencies are not alert and active and that radicals act with

impunity, however, runs contrary to the track record of the administration and its agencies, which, if anything, sometimes seem overzealous and
indiscriminate in their policies and actions.

Similarly, statements that assert that Muslims are not marginalized
and that mainstream Sunni scholars frown upon ijtihad run contrary to
historical facts, court cases, and poll results. Particularly curious is Cohen's
statement: "There is no job discrimination: some senior Bush administration officials, such as Elias A. Zerhouni, head of the National Institutes of
Health (NIH), are Muslims." A Government Accountability Office Report issued in April 2005 noted: "Despite the administration's repeated
pledges of outreach, the State Department's main program directed at the
Islamic world has no Muslim staff, U.S. officials say. 'There's a dearth of
Muslims in the State Department generally,' a senior State Department
official said. Like [Dina] Powell, who is Egyptian American, most Arabs
in the administration are Christians, sources said" (*Washington Post,* April
18, 2005; http://www.washingtonpost.com/wp-dyn/articles/A61213-2005-
Apr17.html).

While there can be agreement regarding the dangers of global terrorism and the need to eliminate or contain it, failure fully to appreciate the
factors that make the war on global terrorism look like a war against Islam
and Muslims contributes both to the growth of anti-Americanism and to
a "clash of cultures" or, perhaps more accurately, a "clash of ignorances."
Graham Fuller is on the mark with his warning regarding the dangers of
American hegemonic policies, pro-Likud or Israeli right-wing forces, and
the rhetoric, theology, and policies of a militant Christian Right (which
I distinguish from the mainstream Christian Right). They constitute an
unholy alliance.

The Bush administration's commitment to promoting democracy in
the Middle East and to resurrecting the Road Map for Peace is laudable.
But it will have to be willing to go further than any previous American administration in pursuing a balanced policy in its dealings with Israelis and
Palestinians, as well as in its democratization policies, to avoid the charge
of operating with a double standard. The antidemocratic policies of many
key U.S. allies in the Middle East and South Asia do not portend well for
the future. This international situation is compounded by domestic policies in Europe and the United States. Antiterrorism legislation as well as
judicial and extrajudicial procedures also reflect a double standard that
erodes long-cherished civil liberties.

Past decades have demonstrated that the methods and ideological
worldviews of many mainstream Islamists (for example, Tunisia's Rashid

Ghannoushi, Iraq's Ayatollah Sistani, the Egyptian Muslim Brotherhood, and various Kuwaiti and Bahraini Islamists) on such issues as democratization, pluralism, and women's rights have developed and changed. Former leaders of Turkey's Islamist Welfare Party became the founders of the non-Islamist, broader-based, and more inclusive AKP.

Abid Ullah Jan and Muqtedar Khan provide good examples of the diversity of Muslim positions. Regrettably, Jan's arguments are too often overwhelmed by unnecessarily provocative rhetoric (the "fascistic American track record," Erdogan as another "Muslim backslider"). Khan's description of moderate Muslims as self-critical, pro-democracy closet secularists (referring here to American rather than French secularism) is significant. American Roman Catholics grappled with similar concerns and made their accommodation, though not without continued problems. An equally important point is Khan's critical distinction: "For moderate Muslims, ijtihad is the method of choice for sociopolitical change and military jihad the last option. For militant Muslims, military jihad is the first option and ijtihad is not an option at all."

Chapter 9

THE ERDOGAN EXPERIMENT IN TURKEY IS THE FUTURE

GRAHAM E. FULLER

RESPONSE TO ARIEL COHEN: In his answer to question 1, Ariel Cohen offers a pretty good definition of a moderate Muslim, which I can subscribe to as far as it goes. The problem comes more with his definition of radical. If all armed resistance to foreign occupation—which over the course of history has had widespread acceptance as a legitimate action—is to be condemned, then of course large numbers of Muslim activists fall into the category of radical. Surely Cohen would not wish to suggest that those guerrilla activities that have led to the founding of countries such as the United States, Israel, Kenya, South Africa, and Algeria via anticolonial struggles are all unacceptable because they passed through a certain violent phase—including elements of what might be terror. I agree with him, as do most Muslims, that in principle killing innocent civilians constitutes an act of terrorism. But that holds true whether it takes place from suicide bombers at a distance of five feet or from five thousand feet when "legitimate government" bombs are dropped on resistance forces and surrounding civilians.

Sadly, much of this debate these days really comes down to the specific tragic events currently unfolding in Israel and Palestine, in which each side seeks the moral high ground for its own version of the issue. If either the Israelis or the Palestinians seek an exclusive monopoly on that moral high ground, then we will lose all moral clarity and will simply be engaged in propaganda exchanges.

The reality is that the current American dragnet of antiterrorism, as well as that of many other countries, sweeps excessively wide in quickly marking individuals as "radical" and hence "dangerous" or "linked to terrorism." Here in this forum we cannot just sift the ideological purity of our favorite radicals or moderates. I would only suggest that if we define politically active Islamists like Tariq Ramadan as "dangerous" and beyond the pale of acceptance for dialogue, then we are indeed defining ourselves out of any serious dialogue with important and influential Islamist leadership. Such narrowness of vision coupled with lack of respect for human rights in the investigation of Muslims has created the widespread impression that the United States is engaged in a "war against Islam." We cannot afford to leave that impression.

Cohen selects a number of individuals that he identifies as moderate Muslims. They are indeed moderate, but they also generally reject all political activity conducted in the name of Islam. Yet it is the majority of individuals on the Islamist spectrum that we need to engage—those who are not themselves violent or creating true hate speech and incitation against an entire class of people but who also do not reject all resistance activity and indeed believe that Islam has something important to say about the way in which Muslim society and governance should be envisioned. If we choose not to deal with such a broad spectrum of people, who occupy important or dominant positions within Muslim society, then we should drop all pretense of dialogue. We no longer have meaningful interlocutors.

In response to Cohen's answer to question 2, my main problem is his characterization of the AKP in Turkey. If non–true believers who vote for a "believers' party" are "opportunists," as he calls them, then an awful lot of "opportunists" voted for George W. Bush. I agree that Turkish Islamists—and any other Islamists—must be careful not to violate secular freedoms. But it is well known that Turkey's "secularism" has actually been the antithesis of any American understanding of the term. Turkish secularism has meant total state domination of religion and the exclusion of religion by law from much of the public sphere. The AKP seeks to permit freedom to wear the hijab (headscarf), currently forbidden in any state institution, including universities, not to impose it. And the AKP seeks to permit graduates of religious schools to be allowed entry to universities, which is currently legally denied, rather than to seek special privileges for them. The party is still learning from its mistakes in some respects. But that is true of most political parties, including the Republican Party that President Bush belongs to.

In regard to his response to question 3, I think Cohen is quite on the mark in his call for greater ijtihad in the understanding of religious texts from a different time and place and circumstances. We are talking not about changing religion but about changing our human understanding of religion.

I largely agree with Cohen's response to question 4, even if not in all details. While the three "Islamist" regimes of the Taliban, Iran, and Sudan have indeed all been disappointing or terrible (like so many other regimes in the Middle East and the developing world), however, it is important to note that all three came to power via an ongoing civil war, a revolution, or a coup. Any regime coming to power under those conditions usually gives short shrift to democracy.

The real test is when an Islamist regime comes to power by the ballot box. The old witticism about "one man, one vote, one time" is actually just that—it does not reflect reality and has never happened yet with an Islamist party. Let us watch the democratically elected Islamists in Turkey, Indonesia, Malaysia, and now Iraq and see what they do about maintaining the democratic order. Frankly, I expect mixed results—some performing well, others not, depending on the conditions, circumstances, and political culture.

As for question 5, I think Cohen is correct about the difficult challenges that face European Muslims both from within the Muslim community and from European societies. I fully agree that it is imperative that Muslim communities everywhere in the West develop their own indigenously raised and educated community members to take over their religious leadership rather than rely upon imams flying in from the Middle East, who generally lack all knowledge of Western society—with all its flaws and virtues. Only then can the Muslim critique of the West be meaningful, and only then can Muslims appreciate what Western values have to offer alongside Muslim values.

I would only point out that the proselytizing instinct runs as deep in Christianity as it does in Islam and that we are all well aware of hateful language about Muslims used even in American texts and public statements on occasion. This is not a uniquely Muslim failing, and we need to condemn all of this, as I am sure Cohen would agree.

RESPONSE TO JOHN L. ESPOSITO: I fully agree with John Esposito's remarks here and his plea for understanding the huge range of Muslim belief and practice in place of the cookie-cutter "good Muslim, bad Muslim" dichotomy that dominates our media and even the views of many top U.S. policymakers today. Indeed, as regards question 2, the problem is above all authoritarianism that both spawns and represses radical and violent Islam.

When local authoritarianism is coupled with occupation and war visited upon Muslim populations, it is little wonder that moderation becomes an endangered species. I believe that Esposito's response to question 3 captures the problems quite accurately.

In regard to Esposito's reply to question 4, I can think of no faster way to sort out the wise from the foolish, the radical from the moderate, and the effective from the demagogic elements among Islamist movements than to allow them gradually to move into positions of responsibility via election to parliaments or other opportunities to take office via the ballot box. They very quickly will have to come up with the goods and convince the electorates that they have the answers. Many of these movements and groups have long had the luxury of sitting on the sidelines offering only criticism or have enjoyed popular backing in their attacks upon authoritarian leadership. Let us make them fish or cut bait. The authoritarians of the region are delaying the Islamist confrontation with reality. Let us see who will pass the test.

Esposito's answer to question 5 is on the mark and accurately identifies the problems and tasks that face Western Muslims. Overall, I am immensely optimistic about the future of Western Muslims and the contributions that they will make both to the West and to Islamic culture. But right now we live in bad times, a circumstance that immensely slows down and complicates the task of creative, imaginative, and activist Muslims in the West.

RESPONSE TO ABID ULLAH JAN: In the context of question 1, Abid Ullah Jan is correct that "moderate" is used in the West to serve different agendas, particularly by self-serving government policies. But I do not think that he rejects outright the very concept of moderate Muslim—even if moderation is incumbent upon all Muslims. Of course, even within the Muslim World different groups use this term for different ends. But ultimately it must be the Muslims who define "moderate" and in what context. Let us not damn the term—some of my best friends are moderates— but rather seek precision about what it means, in whose usage, and to what purposes.

The West cannot be the arbiter of what constitutes Muslim moderation; however, Muslims also need to think about what this term means in practical life and politics. In his response to question 2, Jan raises some significant issues; I concur with many of them, if not perhaps in his precise formulations. The problem of Western domination, colonialism, and neo-imperialism of all kinds poses a massive challenge to Muslim societies, regardless of who is in power. This is an old story of inequality of power throughout history and the de facto reality that "might tends to make right"—in the political, economic, cultural, and geopolitical spheres. Jan is also correct that much of what today passes for a debate over religion is in reality about politics and resistance. The quicker we can get to that level of analysis, the faster we might be able to address some of the real issues between "the West" and "the Muslim World," rather than tilting at unproductive and misleading windmills. In the end, it is stunning that most Western analysis of the problem of "Islam and the West" does not make the tiniest effort to acknowledge even the possibility that Western policies just might have at least something to do with part of the overall confrontation.

But I cannot let Jan glibly write off the Erdogan government in Turkey. It may not represent his exact vision of what an Islamist government should be. But let us not forget that this is the first Islamist party to come to full power via the democratic process in Muslim history. Come on, Abid Ullah, cut these guys some slack! They are making history in Turkey in inching their way, under difficult circumstances, toward a new understanding of what real "secularism" should mean and have carried the torch for not just proposing but actually implementing reform while building respect for the Islamic past and tradition. So far it is working. They are not American patsies. Where else do we see this in the Muslim World? Turkish leaders do not have to be the model for all other Islamists, but they are at least doing a lot that is right. They have gained huge non-Islamist support and are remaking the face of the old Kemalist model (Atatürk was a great hero who rescued the Turks from European imperialism and placed the country on the soundest footing of any Muslim state today, despite many errors, particularly of his latter-day followers). This Erdogan experiment, still in its early days in Turkey, is truly worth watching.

As Jan points out in his response to question 3, the majority of Muslim scholars today are on the government payroll as servants of the state, often as what I call "dial-a-fatwa," when the state wants clerical support for certain policies. Then we have a Muslim World under siege so that the entire culture hunkers down in self-defense to protect its culture from outside attack and intrusion—not a time for liberal thinking in any society. Finally, we have radical extremists who justify all violence in the name of their own reading of Islam. Given this environment, I am not optimistic that any kind of creative ijtihad is likely to emerge. Furthermore, I see too many scholars obsessively concerned with defining what is *haraam* (Islamically forbidden) and with few positive words of constructive thought that will help lead people to God or to rejoice in their human existence.

Of course, the ummah demands a just order, but that is not going to happen anywhere, given the human condition. In the meantime Muslims are likely to engage in their own ijtihad, even unconsciously or without systematic thought, as they strive to live a moral life in a modern world in which they may feel deprived of much guidance. I do not see a lot of broad thinking among Muslim clerics on the grand issues. Instead, they generally focus on narrow concerns. Islam will not survive long into the next century as a vital religion as long as Muslims do not give serious thought to its contemporary meaning. The problem is not Islam, of course, but the human understanding of it.

While it is inappropriate for me as a non-Muslim (but sympathetic to the Muslim World) to comment on how Islam should be understood today, I believe that the weight of scholastic tradition, which frequently consists of scholarly views first propounded a thousand years ago, has often crushed much of the spirit of early Islam in regard to its intellectual vigor and curiosity, tolerance, openness, and inspirational thought. This is where true fundamentalism—getting back to the original meaning and spirit of Islam relative to the time in which the message was enunciated—can serve an especially valuable function in helping to make Islam meaningful to contemporary Muslims.

I would love to see books written by contemporary Muslim thinkers that will command the attention of the world, with something to say to all people on a universal moral level—in the way that so many Protestant, Catholic, Buddhist, Jewish, and other religious thinkers are offering universal messages to the world, which are warmly received by all. Where are the Reinhold Niebuhrs, the Martin Bubers, and the Dalai Lamas of Islam today? Otherwise, for so many Muslims, Islam remains primarily a vehicle of Muslim cultural and social expression. Muslim thinkers should be capable of greater things in this dark world.

I agree with Jan's reply to question 4 about the unconstructive and often destructive way in which the West has interacted with the Muslim World over the past century or two. His last paragraph offers a pious hope for a better future for Muslims, a hope that I share. But I am unconvinced that simply an embrace of the core sources of Islam, defined as the Qur'an and Sunnah, will be enough. These core sources and values have to be rendered in meaningful ways relative to all of the complexities of contemporary life in a manner that permits Muslims to function as an integral part of a universal and global society.

Certainly, American domination of the world in so many spheres affects the nature of that global society. There is much more out there than just the United States, however. Muslims should be powerfully contributing to growing international norms, but they are not. Finally, even if Muslims and their key thinkers embrace the core sources of Islam, these must still be translated into quite concrete and specific formulas—even policies—if they are to demonstrate their relevance. When will Muslim thinkers arise who have something to say that will capture the attention of all Muslims—and beyond? I believe that Muslims are entirely capable of this, but they have not so far done so.

I think that Western, especially North American, Muslims will have a great impact in rethinking the meaning of Islam for contemporary life. As Jan suggests in his reply to question 5, they increasingly have the wealth, the education, the leisure, the security, the freedom, and the means for speaking out.

I agree that the United States is moving in negative directions at this time. It cannot really blame outsiders for this decline, if it takes place. I hope that the present negative trends are just a passing aberration in the wake of the 9/11 trauma. But they may be more than that. If the United States is gradually moving into an era of wholesale decline—a distinct possibility—then it will be in need of its own spiritual reformation.

RESPONSE TO M. A. MUQTEDAR KHAN: I concur with Muqtedar Khan's general view, as expressed in his reply to question 1, on the use and misuse of the term "moderate Muslim." Too often it is used in the United States as a stamp of approval in accordance with the particular foreign policy needs of the moment and America's geopolitical relationship with the state in question.

In general, moderation in any sphere of human life is partly facilitated by the degree of moderation in the environment in which we live. It is hard to be a moderate under conditions of extreme hardship, social and political pressures, or ambient violence—either physical or psychological. If the middle way for Islam or any other religion is to be attained, we require some reasonable degree of good governance, the freedom to reflect and make our moral choices, and also the safety and peace of mind to do so. For the many reasons discussed in this dialogue, these conditions are not often present in today's Muslim World.

While Muslims certainly have the right to determine for themselves what moderate means, the rest of the world (and not just the dominant powers) will also have some views on its meaning as well—on any issue. If words are to mean anything at all at the universal level, there should not be vast disparity among peoples as to what moderate means.

As regards Khan's response to question 2, Turkey is indeed the most promising model in the Muslim World today. It is far from perfect, but it remains the best so far. It does not have to be the only model for Muslims, but its experience is worth studying—not in terms of a predetermined ideological preference, but from a pragmatic point of view. Simply put, Turkey is a Muslim state that functions relatively more successfully than any other and without oil. Why is this so? Various explanations can be offered, but Muslims need to derive some conclusions from this experiment so far.

In terms of secularism, Kemalist Turkey of course has not been secular at all by any American understanding. Rather, it has been a model of state domination of religion with a clear antireligious bias. This is not the ideal for Islam, or most other religions for that matter. But looking back now, perhaps the harsher experience of firm state control over religion, while not desirable, has not been all bad in Turkey. It might have forced Turkish Muslims to refine their ideas about Islam, to build a new understanding about the role of religion in human life. The Turkish experiment is far from over for either its secularists or its Islamists. But it would appear that Turkey, despite all of its problems, is gradually moving toward some kind of democratic social harmony that has so far eluded most other Muslim states. Other Muslims may not like this model entirely, but they still desire that same degree of democratic social harmony.

I could not agree more with Khan's eloquent and considered statement concerning the issues raised in question 3. As for question 4, the jihadi phenomenon springs primarily from the radical and negative character of the sociopolitical life in so much of the Arab world. Muslims, who are angry at their own oppressive regimes and at heavy-handed and ill-conceived American policies, thus often tolerate those advocating radical solutions for radical problems. As Khan suggests, even if they do not support the jihadis' means, they often acquiesce to them and "understand" them, given the radical nature of the problem.

Muslims will be able to take care of extremists of any variety when the extreme conditions that produce them disappear. Muslims will no longer support or even acquiesce to jihadi violence if, in their view, the conditions do not warrant such actions. At that point, dealing with jihadi violence becomes a relatively simple problem for legitimate police and security forces, which enjoy public acceptance.

Only through empowering Muslims to choose their own leadership and policies freely can the blight of violence in the Muslim World begin to decrease. The United States must support this trend toward democracy, even if the tyrant is friendly to Washington. Most smart tyrants seek to be friendly to the United States in order to remain in power and thus contribute to the very problem that produces contemporary violence in Muslim societies.

In his response to question 5, Khan speaks eloquently of the role that American Muslims can play in contributing to and deepening the richness of American life. Muslims everywhere also need to consider the broader lessons that fundamentalist Christians pose. What are those elements that Muslims most object to among the many fundamentalist Christians? It is probably not the Christian theology itself, but the intolerance and the resistance to intellectual, religious, and cultural pluralism in the United States in practice that make Muslims so uncomfortable. How much of a parallel is there between the patterns of thinking and behavior of some Muslim fundamentalists, on the one hand, and the Christian fundamentalist attitudes that disturb Muslims, on the other?

Chapter 10

THOUGH MUSLIMS EXIST TODAY,
ISLAM DOES NOT

ABID ULLAH JAN

COMPARING THE RESPONSES of Ariel Cohen to those of John Esposito and Graham Fuller makes it crystal clear that promoting the concept of moderate Muslims accords with our previously described struggle between the two Americas: extremism versus ideals. This situation is compounded by the self-contradiction and total confusion of the moderates, who, in their desire to cope with the increasingly unreasonable rather than purely un-Islamic standards, wish to appease the extremists in power and attempt to present an Islam that is acceptable to both Muslims and non-Muslims alike.

Instead of elaborating on the supposed "radical ideologies" spread by the "Islamists," the extremists (Cohen) jump to suggesting that they "should not enjoy the constitutional protections of freedom of religion or free speech." Still others suggest that "in the long term ... the legal activities of Islamists pose as much or even a greater set of challenges than the illegal ones."[1] This is an invitation to open fascism. When people are not considered fit even for legal activities, their place in society becomes limited to either the concentration camp or the gas chamber.

The basis of the extremists' preconditions for being a moderate Muslim is the false assertion that Islam is not moderate in the first place. Yet an examination of the criteria being referred to by these non-Muslim paragons shows that many of them do not contradict Islam, which ensures that Muslims are moderate by default. This is aptly shown by their general rejection of terror attacks on fellow Muslims of whichever school of thought as well as on non-Muslims, whether Christian, Jew, or Hindu. Thus there is little reason to append "moderate" to the title "Muslim."

As to the rest of the preconditions, however, these are enough to take the Muslim out of the bounds of Islam. To the extremists, for example, moderate Muslims should:

1. Not "view the greater Jihad as a pillar of faith, or as a predominant dimension thereof."[2]

2. Accept that "the Koran and the Hadith were written for a time and place very different from today" and question the "origins of Islam."[3]

3. Renounce the commands of the Qur'an concerning inheritance, court testimony, and even riba.[4]

4. Consider ijtihad as a tool for innovation, including "rewriting" the Qur'an.[5]

5. Revise the Qur'anic "pronouncements regarding the killing of infidels," as if, contrary to its message,[6] the Qur'an is filled with blind incitements to shed the blood of all non-Muslims for no reason whatsoever.

6. Engage in ijtihad "in parallel with the clear notion of separation of religion and state."

Despite Cohen's notions to the contrary, it is not Islam that is "impoverishing the land of Islam." It should be clear to everyone that no Islamic state exists; ergo, no purely Islamic society exists. The impoverished condition of the Muslims and the violence that some of them resort to have totally different origins, as I have explained (see chapter 5). "Conquering and assimilating 'the other' " (a practice that Cohen ascribes to ancient Middle Eastern societies) is in fact part and parcel of the strategy of enslavement practiced by American extremists.

Cohen and company assume that "political" Islam and Islamic movements pursue "the road of violence." The question is: why should that be? Even if violence has been resorted to in some cases, who initiated the discrimination, deception, violation of the rules, abuse of human rights, and violence in the first place? It is easy to pick on Afghanistan, Iran, and Sudan. No one, however, dares to compare these cases to Israel's history of racism, occupation, the worst kind of apartheid, and ethnic cleansing. There is no reference or comparison to the crimes against humanity committed by non-Muslim governments[7]—not to speak of the 1.8 million murdered by a United Nations–sanctioned genocide in Iraq, the hundreds of thousands killed with nuclear weapons, and the millions still suffering under the tutelage of American-supported tyrannical regimes.

Similarly, a few basic questions require answering to demystify the issue of martyrdom bombings. Who does not love life? What is the state of mind of those who martyr themselves? If it is simply because of some delusional sermons and faulty interpretations, why do Muslims not commit martyrdom bombings in areas other than those under American and Israeli control? If Iraqi "Islamists" want to establish Islam through martyrdom bombing now, why did they not try when Saddam Hussein's regime was much weaker during its last days, rather than under the American occupation today?

The moderates' confusion is exposed when they simultaneously state their adherence to secularism and their commitment to establishing "societies whose organizing principle is Islam" and making Islam "reign supreme in the heart" (chapter 6), knowing that two complete and conflicting systems cannot be in place at one time. How is this goal possible in the presence of secularism's firewall between state and religion? Having Islam as "an organizing principle" means living by Islam in its true sense. Is this realizable in a secular state? Does advocating this mixture of Islam and secularism entail deception of the American extremists, Muslims, or both?

American, British, and French secular laws equally negate the standards by which Muslims are required to live.[8] For example, adultery, prostitution, pornography, gambling, interest (riba), homosexuality, and consuming liquor are not permissible in Islam. A homosexual can bash Christianity or Islam on television, but a Christian or a Muslim cannot speak out against homosexuality. Does this sound like a just society organized according to the principles of Islam?

The moderates who claim to aspire to a society where "communities will compete in doing good, and polities will seek to encourage good and forbid evil" (chapter 6) further undermine their stand for secularism. The salient point is: "encouraging good and forbidding evil" according to whose standards? The principle they cite fits an Islamic society/state more than a secular one. Under the law of Islam, adherents of other religions are not prohibited from conducting both private and public affairs according to their religious laws. Doctrines for legislation and running the state exist that will protect people of all faiths living within the state.

Khan argues that for "moderate Muslims, ijtihad is the method of choice ... and military jihad the last option. For militant Muslims, military jihad is the first option and ijtihad is not an option at all." The logic of the first and last option is as much flawed as the assumption that ijtihad is the exclusive domain of the moderates and that it will always, and only, lead to a state of so-called moderation and modernization. Every Muslim engages in some kind of ijtihad before taking an action; armed struggle is no exception.

Both Muslims and non-Muslims engage in jihad (struggle) and *qital* (war) as well as ijtihad (struggle to reach a right conclusion) for conquests and their domination. What is *fard* (obligatory) is to engage in jihad and qital only to establish Islam, not to gain a piece of land or to rule people. Similarly, ijtihad for legislation according to Islam will only take place when there is an Islamic state.

Esposito and Fuller are considerate but erroneously identify fiqhi Islam as having developed from non-Islamic impulses under monarchies. That is not valid today. Islam is essentially a system of social justice, a politico-socioeconomic order. The model for it, at the highest human level, was demonstrated during the life of the Prophet (peace be upon him) and the Rightly Guided Caliphs: devoid of palaces, empires, and the monopolization of wealth. After *al-khilafah al-rashidah,* Islam went through various periods, with some good rulers and some bad. The good were ruled by Islam, and the bad compromised its ordinances until the disestablishment of the Ottoman state. When the Islamic state is reestablished, however, it will take guidance directly from the Qur'an and Sunnah for legislation. Any pseudo-Islamic state that indulges in fiqh and the practice of traditional Islam will inevitably end up like the Taliban.

The full embodiment of Islam ceased to exist after 1924. Therefore talk of ijtihad is meaningless. The moderates' main confusion concerns the position of ijtihad. Perhaps they are not aware: although Muslims exist to this day, Islam does not. Pervez Musharraf and Irshad Manji also happen to be talking about ijtihad. But in practice they promote non-Islam. Only a revolution on the unique pattern of the Prophet Muhammad (peace be upon him) will provide the answer.

NOTES

1. Jim Lobe, "Anti-Islamic Crusade Gets Organized," IRC Right Web (International Relations Center, March 2, 2005; http://rightweb.irc-online.org/analysis/2005/0503pipes.php).

2. "Demystifying Jihad," Media Monitors.net, May 20, 2004, http://www.icssa.org/Jihad.pdf.

3. Islam is wrongly assumed to be the product of the seventh century, but it is not. See Qur'an 3:84, 38:72, 7:172, and 33:72–73.

4. Daniel Pipes, "Identifying Moderate Muslims," *New York Sun,* November 23, 2004, http://www.danielpipes.org/article/2226.

5. Against Allah's warnings vis-à-vis examples of the past, see Qur'an 2:77–78, 6:144, and 11:110.

6. Qur'an 17:70, 2:256, 5:48, 3:110, and 60:08.

7. R. J. Rummel, *Death by Government* (New Brunswick, NJ: Transaction Publishers, 1994), at http://www.hawaii.edu/powerkills/NOTE1.HTM.

8. Qur'an 5:44–47, 5:78–79, and 9:67.

Chapter 11

MODERATE MUSLIMS ARE THE KEY TO THE FUTURE OF ISLAM AND AMERICAN-MUSLIM RELATIONS

M. A. MUQTEDAR KHAN

I FOUND THAT in Ariel Cohen's responses the devil is, so to speak, in the details. I definitely agree with his understanding of what characteristics constitute a moderate Muslim—eschewing violence and advocating tolerance and pluralism. But when he begins to identify moderate Muslims specifically by name, I find that he mentions individuals who do not exactly represent the mainstream Muslim communities, wherever they are. Does that mean that moderation lies only on the margins of Muslim societies? Surely this is contrary to the more widely held view that a small minority at the margins advocate extremism in the Muslim World, while the vast majority are moderate. This is empirically true everywhere, even in Iraq, where terrorism and insurgency are practiced by a small minority of the smallest minority (Sunnis).

Cohen claims that there is a "near consensus" that Tariq Ramadan is a supporter of the Ikhwan. I am afraid that most Ikhwanis would disagree with this, as would most Islamic modernists who value Ramadan's views. Many prominent scholars of Islam and the Middle East, people who have actually read his books and followed his career, have hailed him as a progressive and moderate voice.

In defense of the American government, Cohen makes two claims. First, he asserts that U.S. government officials are averse to mixing religion and politics. I find this comment surprising, given the extent to which the current administration is allied with the Christian Right and its embrace of faith-based initiatives. Second, I agree with his claim that these same officials are ignorant and incapable of distinguishing between a radical and a moderate. While Bin Laden and al-Zawahiri go free, American government officials are busy harassing prominent moderates like Tariq Ramadan, international peace award-winners like Yusuf Islam, and law-abiding Muslim citizens who go to Canada for a conference.

I agree with Cohen that Islamists must be accommodated under the rubric of a democratic constitution that allows as much room for those who reject Islamism as for those who advocate it. I remain perplexed, however, by his closing remarks in his answer to question 3. He appreciates the value of ijtihad and then argues that—given the Iranian example—it may not be enough. Therefore religion must be separated from politics. If religion is to be separated from politics, then why bother with ijtihad at all? We believe that ijtihad is essential because it allows us to rethink religious sources so that they can have a salutary impact on policy and polity. The idea of Islamic democracy, a major realm of ijtihad today, is premised on the belief that Islamic sources have valuable insights for public policy. I also think that Iran is not a good example for the rest of the Muslim World, since it is primarily Shia and Persian, while the huge majority of Muslims are Sunni and of other ethnicities (prominently South Asian, Malay, Turkic, and Arab). I also agree with Cohen's advice to Muslim leadership to transform its social agenda and focus on education and poverty.

John Esposito, in defining who is a moderate Muslim, makes an interesting point: moderation is not limited to liberal and progressive Muslims—many mainstream Islamists and traditional Muslims also are moderate. I find this observation valuable, because in my own writing I tend to equate moderate Muslims with modernist Muslims. In addition, most progressive voices assume that moderation is their own exclusive preserve. I wish Esposito had pursued this line of discussion in his answer to the question on ijtihad, however.

As a modernist Muslim who privileges the ideas of Muhammad Iqbal and Fazlur Rahman, I lapped up Esposito's discussion of ijtihad and its significance for Islamic revival. While mainstream Islamists and traditional Muslims can be politically moderate, I think that they will oppose ijtihad and the re-understanding of the divine message and will not show any moderation on this score. Esposito, along with most mainstream Muslims, is uncomfortable with applying the term "moderate Muslims" to nonpracticing (secularized) Muslims. In this he departs from the standard tendency within the academy to make no distinction on the basis of religious adherence. I think that this is an important element. Those who desire to be reformist but are not practicing Muslims may not have the legitimacy to reform.

I found Graham Fuller's answers quite balanced. When some angry Muslim asks me, "So who are the moderate Americans?" I usually mention John Esposito and Graham Fuller. I particularly appreciate Fuller's conceptualization of issues in the context of the overwhelming impact of U.S. policies on the Muslim World. I am glad that he emphasizes how great a shadow American power casts on Muslim realities. I wish that he had thought more thoroughly, however, about his assertion of "the absence of intellectual, political, and social freedom within most Islamic societies, except in the West." "Freedom" is a relative term. Muslims enjoy certain freedoms in the West, while they enjoy other freedoms in the Muslim World. No doubt Amina Wadud can feel free and safe to make a major break from Islamic tradition and lead a mixed-gender Friday congregational prayer only in the West. But Tariq Ramadan has been censored and deprived of the freedom to travel, work, and spread his ideas in the United States. Even the poster child of moderate Islam does not enjoy all freedoms in the West. Ironically, Sheikh Yusuf al-Qaradawi enjoys more freedom of speech in Wahhabi Qatar than Ramadan does in the enlightened West. Having said that, I do realize that I would be dead if I lived in certain parts of the Muslim World and wrote what I write (a first-cousin of mine assured me of this).

Abid Ullah Jan, whose arguments are strongly polemical, apparently cannot see anything except the dark side of the West. Even though he maintains that moderation is the normal condition in Islam, he is unable to speak with any degree of clarity about moderation, given that he eschews any discussion of radicalism in Muslim society. He writes as if sectarian violence, terrorism, and jihadism do not really exist. If he believes that all Muslims are moderate by definition, then he should oblige those of us who are obtuse by clearly stating that the jihadi phenomenon is un-Islamic and therefore that all jihadis are non-Muslims. Unfortunately, he saves his criticisms and contempt for moderate Muslims (all of whom he accuses of advancing the agenda of Islamophobic extremist Americans) and provides little or no criticism of the radical phenomenon.

Like those Islamophobes he condemns, who use the example of al-Qaeda and other jihadis to demonize Islam and Muslims, Jan uses Irshad Manji as the exemplar of moderate Muslims to demonize moderate Muslims. There is a near consensus within the Muslim community that Manji is an opportunist playing to the Islamophobic lobby for personal gain;

that she knows little about Islam and Muslims; and that she will have no impact on how Muslims think about Islam in the future. In short, she is irrelevant to the Muslim communities here and abroad. Using her as an exemplar of moderate Muslims is therefore as misleading as using al-Zawahiri as an exemplar of all Muslims.

It is amazing how Cohen and Jan both focus on marginal individuals who enjoy no legitimacy within Muslim communities as examples of moderate Muslims. If we apply Jan's accusations against moderate Muslims, such as a lack of sincerity or knowledge of Arabic and Islamic traditions, in the cases of, say, Tariq Ramadan, Khaled Abou El Fadl (University of California at Los Angeles), Louay Safi (Islamic Society of North America), Asma Afsaruddin (University of Notre Dame), Sherman Jackson (University of Michigan, an example of Esposito's model of the traditionalist-moderate), we find how baseless they are. Jan could study with these extraordinary scholars every day for a decade and still not learn everything that they know about Islamic tradition.

Jan's analysis often seems to be insensitive to empirical and historical facts. For example, he states that the masses in Turkey do not identify with the military regime. What masses? What military regime? A pro-Islamic party (the AKP) is currently in power in Turkey. Jan claims that secular democracies are responsible for genocides. Which secular democracy and which genocide? He makes strong and sweeping accusations without any example or reference, as if he is stating truisms. For someone who makes a lot of brouhaha about tradition, one of his conceptions of ijtihad is very far from traditional jurisprudential understanding. He describes it as part of the process of Muslim struggle for self-determination. I wonder if he realizes that this understanding is closer to the modernist Muslims' understanding of ijtihad than to that of traditionalists.

Based on the participants' positions, it seems readily apparent that—except for dissent from the Muslim radicals—a consensus is emerging that moderate Muslims have a pivotal role to play in the future of American-Islamic relations. It is also evident that many issues besides ideology and security are at stake, the most prominent one being democratization.

{IV}

COMMENTARIES
AND REFLECTIONS
ON THE DEBATE

Chapter 12

IN GOD WE TRUST

The Prospects for the Future of Islam
and the West Are Positive

FEISAL ABDUL RAUF

[QUESTION I] *If moderate Muslims are critical to an American
victory in the war on terror, why does the U.S. government frequently
take steps that undermine moderate Muslims? In your view, who are
these moderate Muslims and what are their beliefs and politics?*

FEISAL ABDUL RAUF (FAR): The debate among the participants shows that
while the term "moderate Muslim" is problematic, we need to define the
attitudinal difference between Muslims who can be worked with and those
who cannot. I suggest that the defining distinction is between those who
believe in a pluralist, multicultural, multireligious societal contract that
allows for differences of opinion within an overarching construct and those
who believe in a societal contract that has no space for other religions,
ethnicities, or cultures or even intra-Islamic differences of opinion.[1]

The attitude of intolerance leads to the phenomenon known as "Islamist terrorism," the modern-day version of the seventh-century Kharijites,
who fought and ultimately assassinated 'Ali, the Prophet Muhammad's
son-in-law, and who over the following century developed a political
philosophy that justified murdering fellow Muslims, including innocent
women and children. Contemporary Muslims need to support that aspect of the war on terror that is a true jihad against all forms of terrorism
(known in classical Islamic jurisprudence as hirabah) and anarchic terrorism that tears the social fabric essential to well-functioning societies. But
this cannot be done without simultaneously purging Muslim societies of
some other modern "isms" that have "terrorized" Muslims and still continue to deny them their inalienable human rights under the Shariah.[2]

One of these is fascism in the Muslim World, whether it has a secular veneer like that of Saddam Hussein in Iraq or an Islamic veneer like that of the Taliban in Afghanistan. Another is nationalism, a modernized form of pre-Islamic tribalism that Muslim theologians call *'asabiyyah* and that more properly belongs to the *jahili* (pre-Islamic) time. This idea can morph into the modern form of Islamic nationalism that, in turn, leads to religious authoritarianism. It oppresses Muslims and non-Muslims who follow authentic and legitimate religious interpretations that dare to differ from the "official" versions and brands anyone who does not accept its point of view as an infidel, thereby arrogating to itself a right that the Prophet declared belongs only to God.

[QUESTIONS 4, 2, AND 3] *What is the future of political Islam, the role of Islam in Muslim society, and required ijtihad in these arenas?*

FAR: A healthy diversity of Islamic political forms exists in the Muslim World. A strong partnership exists in Saudi Arabia between the monarchy and the clergy. In the Islamic Republic of Iran a theocratic rule of the jurisprudent (vilayat-i faqih) prevails. In Jordan the Islamic Action Front (the party established by the Jordanian Muslim Brothers) has accepted and even defended the Hashemite monarchy as legitimate in Islamic terms. In Morocco the Justice and Development Party (PJD) has similarly made its "royalist" credentials very clear in proclaiming its recognition of the king's status as "the commander of the faithful" (*amir al-muminin*). In "republican" Egypt, meanwhile, the Muslim Brotherhood (Ikhwan al-Muslimeen) has endorsed the Islamic credentials not only of the state but also of the government. In Turkey the AKP, currently in government, has similarly made clear its acceptance (and thus in effect its endorsement) of the secularist as well as republican aspects of the Kemalist constitution.[3] In ethnically pluralist Malaysia, where ethnic Malays are constitutionally Muslim and UMNO (the United Malay National Organization) runs the government, Prime Minister Abdullah Badawi ran and won election by the widest historical margin on a platform of "progressive Islam" (*Islam hadari*).

Thus we see that "political Islam," in order to create an operational political space, has accepted and de facto legitimized the nation-state as the framework of its main activity, defining "Islamic state" (*dawlah islamiyyah*) to mean a nation-state where "governance is according to the principles of Shariah." Where political Islam is the "opposition party" to those in power, it has increasingly emphasized other themes—what we may call "ends"—such as the demand for justice (*'adalah*) and freedom (*hurriyyah*). These movements insist on the state's consecration of the Shariah, with two qualifications.

First, these movements realize that Muslims need to "live in harmony with their time," not to re-create the Islamic community of seventh-century Medina. Therefore they stress "the need for *ijtihad*, the intellectual effort of interpretation," to establish how the principles of the Shariah should be translated into legislation in modern Muslim countries.[4] Second, they accept the role of representative assemblies and parliaments in making laws. Islamic political thinking has evolved away from the (originally Kharijite) conception of sovereignty (*hakimiyyah*) as belonging to God alone (*al-hakimiyyah* [or *al-hukm*] *lillah*) to a more or less democratic view that sovereignty belongs to the people.

Therein lies a potential theoretical problem. As Khaled Abou El Fadl points out: "Muslim jurists have argued that law made by a sovereign monarch is illegitimate because it substitutes human authority for God's sovereignty. But law made by sovereign citizens faces the same problem of legitimacy."[5] This leads to the next question: Who is to interpret God's law? In part, this is an issue of power and, in part, of safeguarding the intentions of the Shariah. Otherwise, the power structure uses the mechanisms of the Shariah to undermine and thwart its intentions.[6]

For these reasons, I believe that a coherent "ends" approach that embraces a set of values, as well as an Islamic human rights doctrine that flows out of the Shariah's intent and the core Islamic worldview, is the contemporary demand of history. This is where the determination of an "Islamic state" could currently exert the most traction: Muslim jurists need to come up with an ijtihad road map, list of issues, and methodology—in effect a set of criteria—that could help an audience of lay opinion leaders and those in decisionmaking positions objectively judge what best determines "Islamic" or "Shariah-compliant" governance.

Such an ijtihad would revive spirituality, intellectuality, and ethics, for it would be based on the two commandments common to the three Abrahamic faiths: a love of God and a simultaneous love of our fellow human beings. As a result, this ijtihad would:

1. Revive classical Islam's historic pluralism, an understanding that created space for at least four major Sunni and several Shia schools of legal interpretation to coexist, recognizing them as

equally valid in the eyes of God. Sunni-Shia tensions and the problematic nature of nation-building in Iraq and Afghanistan serve as a metaphor for this uphill challenge.

2. Re-create a nuanced understanding of the difference between separation of mosque and state (which Ali Mazrui has eloquently demonstrated is "Islamically doable") and between religion and politics (not "Islamically doable").[7]

3. Return to what Mazrui has called Islam's authentic spirit of eternal modernism, defined as a continuous creative synthesis: learning from others, letting others learn from Islam, and maintaining Islam's own core of authenticity.[8]

It is also the best antidote to radical groups such as al-Qaeda.

[QUESTION 5] *What impact will Islam have on the West and on Islamic-Western relations? Is the future of Islam and Muslims in the West in danger?*

FAR: I am optimistic about the future of Islam in the West and the relationship between the West and the Muslim World. Western Islamic scholars like those participating in this debate and other Muslim scholars (like Mohammed Arkoun, Ali Asani, Charles le Gai Eaton, Khalid Abou El Fadl, Marnia Lazreg, Martin Lings, Ali Mazrui, Ebrahim Moosa, Seyyed Hossein Nasr and his son Vali, Tariq Ramadan, Abdelaziz Sachedina, Abdul Aziz Said, Frithjof Schuon, Reza Shah-Kazemi, Abdolkarim Soroush, and many, many others who collectively have established a growing virtual diasporic institution of advanced Islamic studies on the important nexus points between Islamic and Western civilization) have contributed and continue to contribute enormously to the intellectual vibrancy of Islamic thought.

We must remember that the United States has had a profound impact on global religion. American Protestantism created a healthy separation between church and state and bequeathed its ideas of pluralism to European Protestantism. American Catholicism influenced global Catholicism, helping bring about Vatican II and its very American ideas about pluralism and church-state separation. American Judaism, by and large, reconfigured world Jewry. It is time for an American Islam that will translate into the Islamic and Western vernacular, for the Muslim and non-Muslim worlds, the best of the United States: its pursuit of the second religious commandment through the benefits of an Islamic democratic capitalism.

In return, the heritage of Islamic civilization has much to offer the West. It could contribute substantially to an expanded cross-cultural dialogue, an enhanced pluralism, and the exploration of new ideas. Islam could make its own invaluable contributions to American understandings of the ideal role for religion and culture in a multiethnic good society. And a healthy Western Muslim perspective is indispensable in mediating differences and improving the relationship between Muslim countries and the United States.

As a pluralist American Muslim, I join Ali Asani in seeing powerful resonance between the pluralism espoused in the Qur'an and the American Declaration of Independence, as well as its Constitution and civic culture, and believe that one can be fully American and Muslim simultaneously. Our loyalty to each demands that we call for certain U.S. foreign policies relating to Muslim peoples and nations to be subjected to critical inquiry and reappraisal and simultaneously challenge intolerant and textually dubious exclusivist interpretations within the Islamic tradition. For in the end our work in bridging the divide between the West and Islam requires both identifying the common high ground and simultaneously struggling against the flaws of the "other," whether that "other" is "the West" or "Islam."[9] Only those within a tradition have the credentials to wage the struggle against its flaws, so American Muslims (namely, those who have assimilated both their American and Muslim dimensions) are uniquely positioned and historically mandated to create the necessary coalitions with non-Muslim Americans on one hand and with non-American Muslims on the other, to correct the flaws lying "within" both the American and the Muslim dimension.

I am grateful to Muqtedar Khan for this opportunity and conclude, in Asani's words, that "in the necessary work of struggling (jihad) against such errors, we should be proud of the best of Islam and of our adopted country, and be inspired by the consonance of their pluralism, and remember the words from the Qur'an that also resonate in the American collective consciousness: In God We Trust (Qur'an 7:89)."[10]

NOTES

1. Until the end of the Ottoman caliphate and the creation of the modern nation-state of Turkey, almost half of Istanbul, two-thirds of Izmir (Smyrna), and large tracts of Cappodocia were Greek. The adoption by Muslim societies of the modern nation-state

paradigm led to the erosion of multiculturalism, which was the norm established by the earliest Muslim rulers, such as Caliph Umar and his successors, based on the Qur'anic teaching that cultural and ethnic diversity is part of the divine plan (Qur'an 49:13).

2. Within seven centuries after the death of the Prophet Muhammad (that is, by the fourteenth century CE), a succession of some of the greatest minds of Islamic jurisprudence, including al-Shatibi, al-Tufi, and others, pointed out that all of the Shariah is designed to further and protect five human rights (called *maqasid al-Shari'ah*): life, religion, family, property, and mental well-being.

3. International Crisis Group, *Understanding Islamism* (Middle East/North Africa Report 37, March 2, 2005, at http://www.crisisgroup.org/library/documents/middle_east___north_africa/egypt_north_africa/37_understanding_islamism.pdf).

4. Ibid., citing International Crisis Group, *Islamism, Violence and Reform in Algeria: Turning the Page* (Middle East and North Africa Report 29, July 30, 2004). Islamist political movements thus reject literalist readings of scripture, taking the perspective of the "Islamic-modernist" movement. Its leading theorist, the Egyptian Muhammad Abduh (1849–1905), attempted to adapt Islamic law in accordance with modern conditions.

5. The nuanced point here is that substituting the absolute sovereign will of the citizens for the absolute sovereign will of a monarch still theoretically overrides the absolute sovereign will of God. This, say Muslim jurists, is incorrect. What is "Islamically correct" is that the worldly sovereign power, whether it resides in a monarchy or in a democracy, must recognize that it needs to be delimited by God as the absolute sovereign. This is the meaning of "acting in accordance with Shariah." In other words, in an Islamic state the worldly ruler (monarch or citizens) cannot be whimsical and must abide by a set of (*shar'i*) principles and fulfill certain objectives that flow from God. In spite of what some modern Americans may believe, the authors of the American Declaration of Independence addressed this very issue in the phrase "one nation under God."

6. El Fadl illustrates this point as follows: "Islamist models, whether in Iran, Saudi Arabia, or Pakistan, have endowed the state with legislative power over the divine law. For instance, the claim of precautionary measures (blocking the means, i.e., *sadd adh-dhari'a*) is used in Saudi Arabia to justify a wide range of restrictive laws against women, including the prohibition against driving cars. This is a relatively new invention in Islamic state practices *and in many instances amounts to the use of Shari'ah to undermine Shari'ah* [italics added]. The intrusive modern state invokes Shari'ah in passing laws that create an oppressive condition—a condition that is itself contrary to the principles of justice under Shari'ah" (*Islam and the Challenge of Democracy*, 15).

7. Ali Mazrui, "Islam between Secular Modernism and Civil Society," a paper presented at the World Economic Forum, Dead Sea, May 2004.

8. In the words of Ali Mazrui: "The Muslim world went modernist long before the West did—but then the Muslim world relapsed back into pre-modernization.... What

made Islam at the time compatible with the spirit of modernity was Islam's own spirit of creative synthesis. Islam was prepared to learn philosophy from the Greeks, architecture from the Persians, mathematics from the Indians, jurisprudence from the Romans—and to synthesize what was borrowed with Islam's own core values. That was a modern spirit … Islam was born pre-modern, but receptive to modernism. Then it went modernist in the heyday of its civilization. Then Islam relapsed into pre-modernism, where it has been stuck to the present day." Mazrui adds, however, that "in the political culture of Muslim Senegal we see signs of the historical proposition that Islam went modernist long before the Western world did. Most of the Muslim world then relapsed into a pre-modernist culture of legalistic lethargy and social conservatism. But even today elements of modernist Islam can be found in unexpected places—from poverty-stricken Bangladesh ready to follow women in hijab as Prime Ministers to post-colonial Senegalese Muslims ready to elect a Christian [Léopold Senghor, a Roman Catholic] for executive President" (ibid.).

9. Ali Asani, "On Pluralism, Intolerance, and the Quran," *American Scholar* 71, no. 1 (Winter 2002): 52–60.

10. Ibid.

Chapter 13

LIBERAL ISLAM VERSUS MODERATE ISLAM

Elusive Moderates and the Siege Mentality

ALI A. MAZRUI

THERE IS A TENDENCY to equate liberal Islam with moderate Islam. Yet on some occasions being liberal demands a sense of outrage and rebellion. The causes of the political radicalization of Islam are different from the roots of theological conservatism. For decades, the Royal House of Saudi Arabia has been theologically conservative but not politically radical. Indeed, for a long time the monarchy in Riyadh was a classic example of how a Muslim regime could be politically pro-Western without being culturally Westernized. Was the Saudi regime politically moderate without being doctrinally liberal?

This debate has been rich in trying to diagnose the nature of Islam's radicalization but relatively thin in diagnosing its causes. The best diagnosis in this collection comes from Graham E. Fuller:

> The Muslim World, feeling itself under siege and with its sensitivities heightened by witnessing the struggle of Muslims across the global *ummah,* is not currently operating in an environment conducive to intellectual openness or liberal and reformist thought. It is simply hunkered down in defensive and survivalist mode. Indeed, the forces of terrorism in the Muslim World must be brought to heel. But that will not happen unless we see a change in hegemonistic U.S. policies, America's explicit embrace of Israeli right-wing policies in the occupied West Bank, and its linkage with fundamentalist Christian attitudes.

I have never heard the problem better formulated. Indeed, there are global causes of Islamic radicalism and global reasons why "Muslim terrorism" has gone international. One factor is the "Latin Americanization" of the Middle East by American policymakers and strategists. Just as Latin America for nearly two centuries had been regarded by the United States as fair grounds for imperial manipulation and periodic military interventions, much of the Muslim World, especially the Middle East, has more recently been treated with similar imperial arrogance. American imperialism in Latin America was an empire of control rather than one of occupation. The same is true of American imperialism in the Middle East.

The second major trigger of globalized Islamic radicalization is the state of Israel, its brutal occupation of the Palestinian lands, the annexation of Jerusalem, and the United States' enormous material, diplomatic, and uncritical support of the Jewish state. The United Nations Security Council cannot even censure Israeli behavior without encountering an American veto. Due to the United States, Israel has been enjoying almost total immunity since at least the 1967 war in the Middle East. The United States provides Israel with an umbrella of impunity. The resulting international frustration has aroused widespread rage throughout the Muslim World.

The third international trigger of Islamic radicalism and major cause of Muslim terrorism is the multiple humiliations of Muslims in so many different countries. Three Muslim countries are under direct foreign occupation (whether acknowledged or not)—Iraq, Afghanistan, and Palestine. Two Muslim populations are under some kind of international trusteeship—Bosnia and Kosova. Several Muslim minorities elsewhere are struggling for self-determination against enormous military odds— including Kashmir, Chechnya, southern Philippines, southern Thailand, and elsewhere. No other civilization in the contemporary world is under a comparable sense of siege. This is quite apart from lower-intensity rivalries between Muslims and non-Muslims in Nigeria, the Ivory Coast (Côte d'Ivoire), and Ethiopia. (I regard the conflicts in Sudan as more Arab versus less Arabized rather than Muslims against non-Muslims.) Politically and militarily, the Muslim ummah is more sinned against than sinning.

Almost all of the contributors to this debate agree that Muslim radicalization has domestic causes as well as global causes. Such domestic causes include authoritarian Arab monarchs and other undemocratic Muslim regimes. But even those domestic radicalizing forces might not have risen to levels of terrorism if they were not reinforced by a resentment of American support for most Muslim dictators for decades—especially oil-rich dictators, but also oil-poor Pakistan and Egypt. Pro-democracy forces in countries like Egypt, Pakistan, and Saudi Arabia were enough to politicize Islam and even to radicalize it. But the rise of the temperature to the level of terrorism is almost always ignited by anti-Americanism or anti-Westernism, even at the domestic level.

I am not a moderate Muslim in the American sense of moderate. Yet at least on three issues I regard myself as a liberal Muslim: I am against the death penalty, I am in favor of gender equality, and I believe that ijtihad will become increasingly crucial as a solution to Islam's doctrinal problems. I came out of the closet on the death penalty during the uproar over Salman Rushdie's *The Satanic Verses* in the 1980s. I deplored the book, denounced the author, and dissented from the death penalty not just for Rushdie but also for anybody else, regardless of the offense.

On gender equality, I have experienced qualified reservations about polygamy but not outright rejection. I grew up in a polygamous family and know its strengths as well as its weaknesses. But I have supported Amina Wadud's effort to end male monopoly of religious leadership. I began to support her effort long before she dramatically demonstrated it by leading a Friday prayer in New York City in March 2005. She had attempted it in a mosque in Cape Town, South Africa, in the 1990s, but with only limited success. I cheered her even then.

LIBERAL ISLAM ON THE DEFENSIVE

But those of us who see ourselves as liberal Muslims are greatly hampered by the external forces of Zionism, the American imperium, and the global humiliation of Muslims from Kashmir to Chechnya. Once again, Graham E. Fuller captures the fundamentals: "As long as conditions in the Muslim World remain radicalized—by terrorism, the sweeping U.S. military response, dictatorship across the region, and a sense of Islam under siege— only radical groups will flourish. Moderation and liberalization can only flourish in a quieter and freer environment, where radical voices find a limited response."

In this paragraph Fuller almost equates liberalization with moderation. In the literature about developing countries, there was a time when modernization was equated with Westernization. To be "modern" was to be as "Western" as possible. In the literature about Islam, more recently, the concept of moderation has come close to being equated with Westernization. To be "moderate" is now translated as being as "Western" as possible. Sometimes the concept "liberal" is also hijacked by the West.

But most African social scientists and thinkers, for example, nowadays would reject the proposition that the modern African society is necessarily the Westernized African society. What about thinkers of the Muslim World? Do they accept the proposition that the moderate Muslim society is the Westernized ummah? These are precisely the equations that make the reforms of Muslim liberals so difficult to implement in a broad climate of Islamophobia in the Western world and a deepening Americophobia in the Muslim World. Muslims begin to lose their moderation.

Muqtedar Khan would surely agree that anti-Western sentiment in the Muslim World is not necessarily anti-Christian. Al-Qaeda's strategy of September 11, 2001, seemed to target the economic symbol of American power—the World Trade Center, which they destroyed. Al-Qaeda also appeared to target the military symbol of American power—the Pentagon. The airplane that crashed in Pennsylvania seems to have been intended for either Capitol Hill or the White House, symbols of American political power. What was missing on September 11, 2001, was any attempt by al-Qaeda to target a cathedral in either Washington or New York as a symbol of American religiosity.

Al-Qaeda succeeded in demolishing a symbol of American economic might in New York. It triumphed in damaging a symbol of American military hegemony in Washington, D.C. Since the passengers in a fourth plane successfully overcame the Muslim warriors, al-Qaeda failed to hit a symbol of American political power. What al-Qaeda never targeted at all was a symbol of American Christian faith.

All of the contributors to this debate find a place for ijtihad—a "juristic tool" and potential mechanism of reform. John L. Esposito gives ijtihad a wide role, whereas Abid Ullah Jan narrows its scope. My position may lie somewhere in between the views of these two colleagues; however, my reasons may be somewhat different. Ijtihad may make Muslims more liberal but not necessarily more moderate. My central thesis in this regard is that God deliberately reveals Himself in installments, partly through religious messengers and partly through the march of science and expanding human experience. Some of the experiences may be radicalizing rather than moderating.

Human History as Divine Revelation

Islam recognizes so many prophets (*nabiyyun*) and so many messengers or apostles (*rusul*) because Allah reveals Himself in such installments across time and across space. The Prophet Muhammad was the last prophet (*nabi*), but was he the last messenger (*rasul*)? Let us accept that he was also the last rasul in the form of a human person. But could Time be a continuing cosmic rasul or at least a *risalah* (messengership)? Is history a continuing revelation of God? Is expanding science a noncarnate rasul?

If God reveals Himself incrementally, and if history is a continuing revelation of God, should we not reexamine Muhammad's message in the light of new installments of Divine Revelation? The Muslims of the first Islamic century would not have understood much about distant galaxies. So Allah talked to them in simple terms about our own moon (as if it was the only moon) and about the sun in the Milky Way (as if it was the only sun). Fourteen centuries ago, the Almighty as the creator of our own galaxy overwhelmed the Arabs. Today we know that God created billions of galaxies. Should we not reinterpret the Qur'anic verses on the sun and the moon in the light of our new understanding of astronomy and the cosmos?

If we need to reinterpret these verses on astronomy, why can we not reinterpret Islamic verses about ancient punishments (*hudud*)? The expansion of human knowledge is not only about the stars. It is also about human beings themselves and their behavior. If we now know more about the causes of crime, we also know more about the limits of culpability and guilt. We know that poverty, bad parenting, a sense of injustice, racial discrimination, a chemical imbalance in the human body, a bad neighborhood, and a bad social environment can all be contributing factors that turn a human being toward crime. At times ijtihad can lead to both liberalization and moderation.

From these conclusions, I proceed to the belief that some verses were about events during the Prophet's own time and that other verses were eternal in purpose. We can illustrate this with the verses about Abu Lahab ("father of the flame"). I believe that the Prophet's contemporaries knew that the verses were about the Prophet's uncle, 'Abd al-'Uzza ibn 'Abd al-Muttalib. In the Prophet's own time, it was understood that the verses were about a specific individual enemy of Islam. Should we reinterpret "Abu Lahab" in a more timeless fashion? Alternatively, should we be reinterpreting verses in ways that would make them historically specific?

The Sudanese theologian Mahmood Muhammad Taha argued about Islam's two messages: the time-specific and the eternal message. The government of Jaafar Nimeiri executed him in 1985 in the name of Islamic hudud. Please read his *The Second Message of Islam* (Syracuse University Press, 1987; paperback 1996; originally written in Arabic and later translated into English). Taha was a force for doctrinal liberalization rather than political moderation.

If God has been teaching human beings in installments about crime and punishment, and if police, prisons, forensic science, and knowledge about genes did not exist fourteen centuries ago, the punishments had to be severe enough to serve as deterrents. Hence the hudud. Since then God has taught us more about crime, its causes, the methods of its investigation, the limits of guilt, and the much wider range of possible punishments. Did the Prophet Muhammad not say: "My people will never agree on error"? If so, we can take it for granted that Muslims of the future will be less and less convinced that amputating a hand is a suitable punishment for a thief under any circumstances. This is a prediction. I have not the slightest doubt that the Islam of our grandchildren will never accept penal amputation of a thief's hand as legitimate. On such issues, doctrinal liberalism converges with social moderation.

Abid Ullah Jan rightly salutes the Companions and the Prophet's disciples. We revere them as the first converts to Islam and as supporters of our Prophet (peace be upon him). But we must not forget that they were not themselves prophets; most of them were not even saints. As ordinary human beings, they were the usual mixture of vices and virtues. That is why three of Islam's first four caliphs were assassinated and why there was an Arab civil war within little more than a decade after the Prophet's death—with 'A'ishah, the Prophet's widow, fighting 'Ali, the Prophet's cousin and son-in-law! The Companions' behavior was often neither liberal nor moderate. Have we been idealizing them too much?

If the Prophet's disciples could be fallible, so could the founders of the Islamic legal schools. Indeed, for fourteen centuries the Qur'an and hadith have been interpreted almost exclusively by men. Male-centrism has also been a historic feature of Judaism and Christianity. There is enough in the Qur'an to support gender equity, but none of the four Sunni schools was founded by a woman. It might have made a difference if one legal school had been founded by a woman like Amina Wadud. Such a female theologian could be a voice of liberalization rather than of moderation.

The Qur'an does not prohibit slavery (any more than do the Bible and the Torah), but the Qur'an goes further than its sister religions in encouraging the freeing of slaves. Islam is not antislavery, but it is pro-emancipation. If early Muslims had used ijtihad enough, the abolitionist movement would have started in the Muslim World a thousand years before William Wilberforce, John Brown, or Abraham Lincoln.

Many other humane gems in the Qur'an are waiting to be fully revealed through ijtihad. Some may enrich liberal thought without encouraging political moderation. But current Islamic thought is indeed "mired in literalism, narrowness of vision, and intolerance" (to quote Fuller). The necessary climate for an Islamic renewal is hampered by the forces that have put Islam on the defensive. Both political moderation and doctrinal liberalization among the Muslim masses will remain difficult as long as the United States remains imperial and Islamophobic in foreign policy, Israel continues to brutalize the Palestinian population and occupy territory, and the rest of the world permits the humiliation of Muslims from Chechnya to Afghanistan, from Kashmir to Iraq. When Muslims are politically radicalized, they often tend to be resistant to doctrinal liberalization. The ultimate causes of radicalization are primarily non-Muslim in origin. But the Muslim World suffers the most from the excesses of both political radicalism and doctrinal conservatism.

Chapter 14

REFLECTIONS ON IJTIHAD
AND MODERATE ISLAM

LOUAY SAFI

MY REMARKS FOCUS on two central themes addressed in the preceding debate: moderate Muslims and ijtihad. Although my assignment requires me to engage the five illustrious interlocutors, I have chosen to refer to salient aspects of their statements, particularly those that help in clarifying the two themes alluded to above. Given the brevity of my remarks and the limited space allocated to comments, it is not possible to expound on the epistemological and ontological underpinnings of the debate. The following arguments therefore take the form of a number of assertions that lack theoretical grounding. Readers who do not share the basic assumptions upon which the arguments are premised may be surprised at these assertions, but I guess this is exactly what the editor intended: to explore diverse views inside and outside the Muslim community.

Still, this intellectual exercise provides an important backdrop for the current debate about the significance of Islam in the profound transformations occurring in contemporary Islamic thinking. I also believe that the debate reveals the complexity of the process of Islamic reform and diversity of its forms and manifestations.

MODERATE ISLAM

"Moderate Islam" has become a most contentious term, as this debate shows. The word "moderate" is frequently used in reference to the political centrist: a person who takes a position in the political center. A moderate is a person who is neither on the extreme left nor on the extreme right of the political, moral, or religious spectrum of ideas.

Defining "moderate" becomes tricky when we take a historical view of mainstream society. From a historical point of view, the terms "moderate" and "extremist" immediately lose their absolutist standing and acquire a relativist sense. Being a Christian and subscribing to Christian values and beliefs was considered extreme in Roman society until Emperor Constantine's time. So was the moral position that "black people and women were equal to white men" in the United States during the eighteenth and the better part of the nineteenth century.

Recognizing the divergence between social and moral moderation and the need to listen to unpopular views and engage off-center positions, democratic societies have adopted apolitical and amoral definitions of moderation. From a democratic point of view, a moderate is one who does not resort to violence or intimidation to achieve political goals. The emphasis here is not on beliefs and values but on the approach to dealing with political and moral conflicts. Those who resort to intimidation and imposition to advance their views and values are extremists, even when the majority may judge their values and beliefs to be moderate. Conversely, those who respect the equal dignity of others, even when they disagree with them, must be considered moderate from a democratic point of view. Voltaire epitomized this democratic spirit, which defines the moderate stance in modern society: "I disagree with what you say, but I will fight to the death to protect your right to say it."

The term "moderate Muslim" is now being used by anti-Muslim groups in the West as a weapon to delegitimize and isolate critical Muslim voices. The "moderate Muslim" par excellence is a person who is not comfortable with his/her Islamic roots and heritage, is openly hostile to Islam, and is eager to transcend all Islamic norms. Irshad Manji became a Muslim voice of moderation after she repudiated all things Islamic in her book *The Trouble with Islam: A Muslim's Call for Reform in Her Faith* (New York: St. Martin's Press, 2004). The title "moderate" was also conferred on Muhammad Hisham Kabbani after he testified before a congressional committee that extremists control more than 80 percent of American mosques. Both Manji and Kabbani are seen as moderates, even though their views on social issues are far off-center as regards the American and the Muslim mainstream communities. Both represent fringe views within the Muslim community and hardly speak on issues of concern to American Muslims or Muslims worldwide.

Ariel Cohen sees Tariq Ramadan, an authentic European Muslim voice, as a misconstrued "moderate." Cohen points to a "near consensus" that Ramadan has already crossed the boundary of moderation, based on the account of his positive interaction with Muslim scholars who stand on the wrong side of the Israeli-Palestinian conflict (most notably Yusuf al-Qaradawi), a misconstrued association with the Ikhwan, and his alleged anti-Semitism.

Never mind that Ramadan has been a critic of the Ikhwan, a critic of anti-Semitic expressions in Arab and Muslim society, and a proponent of integrating Islam and Islamic values into Western culture.

Indeed, there is near consensus among pundits who define moderation on the basis of categorization as a consistent supporter of Israel or the Likud party, or the lack of it, that Ramadan is an anti-Semite. What is rarely discussed is that this label stems from a confrontation between Ramadan and a group of French intellectuals that he had criticized for not repudiating the Likud government's policy toward the Palestinians. I do not intend to discuss Ramadan's case here, because a fair discussion would require a space beyond the scope of my current task. I would rather underscore an important point: the efforts to dismiss authentic Muslim voices when they express views critical of U.S. foreign policy or Israeli policies in the West Bank and Gaza violate the essence of democratic politics.

We must all recognize that attempts to intimidate and marginalize voices critical of Israel and American foreign policy are antidemocratic and extremist. Therefore I fully agree with Graham Fuller that the term "moderate Muslim" is subject to an unrealistic litmus test regarding views on Israel that excludes the majority of serious Muslim voices, thereby dismissing potential interlocutors. I would add that such isolation tactics work both ways in a world in which the United States increasingly finds itself unable to sustain its unilateralist approach to world politics.

American Muslims bring fresh voices and unique experiences that are very needed in the West. Their voices are essential for developing a well-informed public opinion able to promote world peace, an undertaking in which the United States continues to play a positive role. These voices may not be popular, but they are crucial to preventing the increased schism between Western and Muslim societies. The efforts to isolate them constitute an unfortunate and ill-conceived posture and are likely to contribute to further isolation of the United States, as its foreign policy becomes more reliant on self-perception instead of the real facts on the ground.

IJTIHAD AND INTELLECTUAL DEVELOPMENT

Ijtihad refers to consistent intellectual endeavors to relate universal Islamic values and principles to changing sociopolitical circumstances. It also refers to various scholars' intellectual efforts to study Islam's normative sources in order to identify the universal principles behind particular moral annunciations and then reapply these principles to evaluate current societal institutions as well as to suggest possible reforms to bring actual practices in line with Islamic ideals. As such, ijtihad goes beyond juristic reasoning and takes the form of creative thinking in various fields in human experience. Hence Khan's distinction between juristic and nonjuristic ijtihad is quite relevant to contemporary discourse. In addition, this understanding makes ijtihad central to any attempt to undertake reform in Muslim society.

The most serious obstacle for reform in Muslim society has been the attempt to impose on Muslim societies various institutions and practices that were developed in the modern West. The failure to root modernization and development in the moral values and historical experiences of Muslim society has generated suspicion, resentment, and resistance. As a result, progress and development have been retarded.

The emergence of a vibrant American Muslim community provides contemporary Islamic reform efforts with a unique opportunity to bring Islamic values and principles to bear on modern society. Not only does North America provide a markedly greater freedom to undertake a genuine reform, but it also forces Muslims to undertake a fresh reading of Islamic sources and to separate the cultural (and hence the particular) from the universal elements of Islam. The divergence between forms of social life in the modern West and historical Muslim societies leaves no room for the blind imitation of past institutions and approaches.

Given this, I find Abid Ullah Jan's concerns about the distortion of Islam unwarranted. Jan generalizes from unfortunate instances of Muslim intellectualism, *a là* Irshad Manji, who espouses a static and reductionist understanding of the Islamic legacy and hence contributes to the distortion and misrepresentation of the Islamic spirit. But this is generally the exception rather than the norm. Muslim-bashers who are eager to embrace any voice that validates their distorted views of Islam and Muslims have made it extremely tempting for those Muslim opportunists who are just dying for attention and who fail to distinguish between fame and notoriety.

During the twentieth century, contemporary Islam underwent remarkable reforms, including reform undertaken by intellectuals who had no formal juristic training. It is interesting to note that the least renewal and development in Islamic thought has taken place within juristic thinking, thanks to the failure of most contemporary jurists to distinguish between change as corruption and change as improvement and development.

Islamic thinking has developed and matured remarkably on the social, political, and economic levels, but far less on the legal and juristic levels. As contemporary Muslim thinking continues to mature and develop, more attention must be given to juristic thinking, because the notion of Islamic law in modern society continues to lag behind. To a large extent, this may be attributed to the prevalence of an analogical mode of thinking and the retreat of the purposive mode of thinking. The distinction between these two modes is what John Esposito describes when he contrasts the principles of qiyas (analogy) and istihsan (equity).

Analogical thinking looks into the particular reason behind the Qur'anic or the prophetic text and extends the application of the Shariah to all instances that share in the same reason. According to this way of thinking, a trade contract involving products that have not been manufactured (*'aqd al-istisna'*) is unlawful because the Prophet prohibited such transactions. Purposive thinking moves from the reason to the purpose and thus allows this transaction if fraud can be avoided and the right of the buyer can be guaranteed. Purposive reasoning not only ensures that the Shariah is more accommodating but also that its overarching purposes (such as equity, human dignity, freedom of religion, and protection of individual rights) are not compromised when enforcing various Shariah rulings.

Chapter 15

CULTURE TALK

Six Debates That Shape the Discourse on "Good" Muslims

MAHMOOD MAMDANI

IN HIS BOOK *Persecution and the Art of Writing* (Glencoe, IL: Free Press, 1952), Leo Strauss, the University of Chicago political philosopher, analyzed the technique of writing under repression. He discussed medieval philosophers who had written under repression (al-Farabi, Maimonides, and Spinoza), but this was not an esoteric exercise. The cold war had begun only three years before, and American officialdom tended to see a Communist behind every book. "In a considerable number of countries which, for about a hundred years, have enjoyed a practically complete freedom of discussion," wrote Strauss, "that freedom is now suppressed and replaced by a compulsion to coordinate speech with such views as the government believes to be expedient, or holds in all seriousness" (p. 22).

Persecution, Strauss noted, "gives rise to a peculiar technique of writing," "in which the truth about all crucial things is presented exclusively between the lines" (ibid., p. 22). But what if only some are conscious of the growing repression and thus write between the lines, while most have so internalized the repression as common sense that they translate it into a narrow agenda? Surely, in such a case, the most appropriate response is to broaden the parameters of the discussion in order to read not just between the lines but also beyond the margins. In what follows, I try to do so by identifying and commenting on the issues driving the debate between participants.

DEBATE ONE: CULTURE AND POLITICS

One of the most amazing news items that I read in the weeks following 9/11 was in the *New York Times:* sales of the Qur'an had soared in the

United States as more and more Americans sought to read it for clues as to what had motivated the hijackers. In the months and years that followed, I wondered if the people of Afghanistan or Iraq, even of Fallujah, were reading the Bible for an explanation for the bombs raining upon them from on high. I doubted that any of them really did. What could explain this difference?

I am convinced that the difference lies in how the public debate on 9/11 has been framed by public intellectuals in the United States. Most public intellectuals, especially the quasi-official ones, share assumptions that I call culture talk. The core assumption is that we can read the politics of some people—those who are not "modern"—from their culture, for they do not make their culture; rather, it is their culture that makes them. Even those who accept that all cultures are historical assume that cultures grow in separate containers called "civilizations" that talk and exchange but only do so at the margins. Because they all develop along the same lines, we can tell who is more and who is less developed. In addition, it is characteristic of the less developed that they require an external impulse to get out of a vicious circle. The historical responsibility of the more advanced culture, then, is either philanthropy—to bring "development" or "democracy" to those less fortunate—or policing the world by imposing a quarantine on those likely to act out of resentment or anger.

Culture talk has a history. It is about taking the moral high ground and is as old as colonialism. Democracies have always had to justify colonialism to their populations as a selfless and philanthropic endeavor. Not surprisingly, the justificatory literature on colonialism typically identifies vulnerable groups in the target countries—those who need to be saved—and turns them into so many proxies. This is how we need to understand the nineteenth-century British preoccupation with the talk of saving Indian women (by ending practices like *sati,* polygamy, and widow marriage) and children (by ending child marriage) or entire populations in Africa from possible enslavement, as well as the contemporary American preoccupation with female genital mutilation. It used to be called "the White Man's Burden"; now it is called "humanitarian intervention."

This is also how we need to understand the blatant double standards practiced by official America today: permissive toward its allies and clients, while calling for adversaries to be held accountable. As a result, death in Darfur is termed genocide and calls for a global response, whereas the killing of many more (over 3 million by the most conservative count) in the eastern part of the Democratic Republic of the Congo is a regional tragedy somehow unworthy of wider concern and the arraignment of over a million citizens in northern Uganda is an internal problem. Most culture warriors have a romantic view of homeland cultures. Those Americans who are preoccupied with the urgent need to reform other societies are often blissfully silent about the sea change in American politics and society over the past few decades. With religious study circles spreading in official Washington circles, chances are that most political extremists with a religious orientation—whether jihadi or not—would find the United States' governing institutions very congenial places in which to formulate policies to remake the world.

Culture talk is self-serving in yet another way. If people slap me and I explain it as an expression of "their" culture, it removes me from the picture. To explain a development like 9/11, we need to focus on relationships between those central to the event. And that means shifting the focus from culture to politics.

Debate Two: The Internal vs. the External

All cultures are historical. But even if it is understood as historical, is culture a wholly internal category? What is the relationship between the "internal" and the "external" in the politicization of cultural and religious identity? Modernity tends to politicize culture. Take the example of that very modern empire: the Ottoman Empire. The Ottoman millet system created a form of "indirect" rule that went far beyond the tendency of earlier empires simply to impose fiscal and military demands through unequal relations with the conquered territories. In also recognizing the religious community as a political entity, the Ottomans recognized religious authority as political and sanctioned new powers (for example, of taxation and adjudication) for that authority. Instead of practicing a form of overrule that did not disturb internal relations, Ottoman authority politicized and transformed internal relations. In the mid-nineteenth century the Dutch and the British would arrive at a similar form of rule. They politicized different types of cultural communities, however: religion here and ethnicity and caste there.

For Europeans, the politicization of culture began right at home as nation-states replaced multinational empires. In the new modern European empires, the politicization of culture became a more efficient technology of rule, a way to divide and rule whole peoples instead of just elites. Faced with a resistance that they were unable to put down for over two decades in Aceh, the Dutch finally decided to create another form of authority parallel to the ulama—the authority of chiefs—and sanction it as "traditional." The result was two parallel authorities with two different (and possibly conflicting) sources of legitimation: one anchored in custom (*urf*) and the other in religion (the Shariah).

The British also set aside their ambitions to "civilize" native peoples by bringing them under the rule of (English) law. Faced with resistance at two ends of the empire, in the West Indies and India, in the mid-nineteenth century, they looked for "traditional" allies. Queen Victoria's declaration in 1858, after the Sepoy Mutiny of 1857, that the Crown would not interfere in "religion" gave it the power to determine and to police the boundaries and the authorities of "religion." Those who want to understand the Shariah and the debates around it in pre-partition India would do well to historicize their understanding of Anglo-Mohammedan law. The same thing can be said of implementing (ethnic) "customary" law and authority in Africa.

Empires, whether local or colonial, had little appetite for a type of law that would recognize different interests in the form of divergent interpretations. Whether the law was "customary" or "religious," they looked for a single infallible source of interpretation. If it did not exist, they created it. So both the British and the Dutch claimed that any change in "tradition" or "custom" was prima facie evidence of its corruption. We need to keep in mind that such a claim would never be made about "tradition" at home. In the colonies, however, "genuine" tradition was said to have two characteristics: first, it must not change; and second, it must be enforced through law.

I have gone through this long diversion on modern empires and colonialism to make one point: we need to understand both the politicization of culture (and religion) and the hardening of internal relations in the historical context of an encounter between Western power and non-Western societies. The polemic between what is external and what is internal is not particularly useful; nor is the notion of all cultures developing through containers called "civilizations," each of which is external to the other. It is not just that the lines between civilizations are porous and have become blurred; rather, what was an external imposition at the start of a historical period came to be internalized during its course.

DEBATE THREE: THE QUESTION OF SECULARISM

The parameters of the present debate on Islam and secularism were set by Princeton Orientalist Bernard Lewis, first in his 1990 *Atlantic Monthly* article "The Roots of Muslim Rage" and then in his book *What Went Wrong* (New York: Harper Perennial, 2003), in which he rehashed these same ideas. Lewis claimed that the problem with Islam was that it never success-fully made the transition from theocracy to secularism, as the West did—which is why, he said, Muslim fundamentalists are at war with secularism and modernity. Even more revealing of his political agenda was his claim that the Islamic critique of the West was similar to fascism, communism, and "third worldism." Lewis's ideas have generated two kinds of responses. The first has internalized the key assumption of his argument: there is in-deed a single Western experience (with no significant internal variations), which represents the norm (the universal) that all others must duplicate or turn into so many abnormalities. This response goes on to claim that Islam is just as secular and modern as the West.

In contrast, the second view questions Lewis's assumption and points out the need to understand that human development is diverse and that this diversity is the outcome of multiple paths of historical development. Thus it is necessary to understand the specificity of historical development in Islamic societies, particularly how the boundary between religion and the state has developed and functions.

I find the second kind of response far more productive and illuminat-ing. The key contribution comes from Reinhard Schulze (*A Modern History of the Islamic World* [London: I. B. Tauris, 2002]), who points out the need to grasp the historical fact that in Islam there is no "religious power that had to be separated from worldly power." Whereas historical Catholi-cism developed as the prototype of the empire state, and historical Protes-tant denominations as the prototype of the nation state, Islam contained no institutionalized religious power. Thus one question that is central to secularism—namely, delineating the boundary between religious and sec-ular power—has been a nonquestion in historical Islam.

The significance of this can be seen in the development of state power in Islamic societies. Whereas both political power and social practices in Islamic societies have been particularly wanting in tolerating "internal" differences (for example, relating to the rights of women, nonbelievers, and divergent sects), their historic strength has been the tolerance of "ex-ternal" diversities, because they did not automatically see these as political threats. This particular historical line of development also explains why it has been so easy for secular thinkers to cross the boundary into the religious domain in Islamic societies and why key theoreticians of radical political Islam have tended to come from the secular sphere. It also makes sense of Richard Bulliet's observation in *The Case for Islamo-Christian Civilization* (New York: Columbia University Press, 2004) that religious scholars in Islam have traditionally played the role of checking the ruler's absolute power in the name of justice (rather than liberty). Indeed, as Bulliet points out, the most tolerant expressions of Islamic faith today come from those trained in traditional religious schools, not from those with training in secular subjects.

This perspective also makes sense of the one major (and recent) exception to this trend—Ayatollah Khomeini's construction of clerical power as vilayat-i faqih—as a preemptive move in the face of challenge from secular thinkers like Ali Shariati. For those tempted to see Khomeini's innovation as a Shia norm, we only have to point out that it is currently under great stress not only from the democratic movement in Iran but also from rival theological interpretations, as signified by the alternate conception associated with Ayatollah Sistani: that the clergy must be a moral/political force outside the state rather than a force within the state.

DEBATE FOUR: THE ROOTS OF JIHADI ISLAM

Jihadi Islam identifies Islam with a single pillar, jihad, and then proceeds to offer a reinterpretation of it. Key to this debate is jihadi Islam's embrace of violence as central to political and social change. How are we to understand the development of jihadi Islam as a theoretical (or theological) tendency? Can its particular understanding of the Qur'anic text be illuminated by the historical context of its development? In answering "yes" to this question, I found it most useful to trace this development as the history of an idea, most recently through two important post–World War II theorists of political Islam: Abu Ala al-Maudadi and Sayyed Qutb.

Crossing the boundary from post-partition India to Pakistan, Maududi was aghast at how banal he found the Muslims of Pakistan; nothing but rituals seemed to distinguish them from the Hindu population of India. His loss of confidence in everyday Muslims went alongside his formulation of Islam as a state project: they would have to be made into Muslims. Islam is not a mere religion; it would have to be a *din* (like communism, he says at one point), meaning a state ideology. Maududi represents the point of a radical shift in political Islam, from a society-centered (with a focus on the ummah) to a state-centered ideology.

Is it simply incidental that the shift in political Islam occurs alongside a similar shift in other forms of nationalist thought in the postcolonial period, from a society-centered to a state-centered perspective? Sayyed Qutb is notable from this point of view, in that he introduces the distinction between "friend" and "enemy" (see his *Signposts* [Indianapolis: American

Trust, 1990]): we must use reason with friends and force with enemies. This distinction resonates with many other radical perspectives of the period, so to speak, across the board. Are we to understand Maududi and Qutb as simply thinking inside a tradition—political Islam—or as also being engaged in conversation with competing contemporary ideologies of national liberation (particularly secular nationalism and Marxism-Leninism), with which they shared a number of characteristics, including a growing faith in political violence?

My point is that the contemporary jihadi Islamist embrace of political violence must be understood as a modernist project, not as a premodern leftover in modernity. Violence has been at the heart of political modernity: at least since the French Revolution (1789), modern people have thought of violence as central to progress. Karl Marx's dictum that revolution is the midwife of history is part of this modernist perspective. No other century was as preoccupied with progress as the twentieth, and none more violent. But we need to remember that those who lived during that century were likely to think of most violence (revolutions, world wars) as "good" and not "bad" violence.

This understanding can illuminate the history of the cold war for us. When George Kennan came to write an op-ed in the *New York Times* toward the end of his life, he lamented that even though Western powers had already achieved containment in the first few years of the cold war, they kept it going out of their determination to bring the Soviet Union to its knees no matter what the cost. Ronald Reagan epitomized this point of view and rationalized it by politicizing a religious vocabulary. The Soviet Union, he said, was "an evil empire"—and there could be no coexistence with evil. Evil had to be destroyed; coexistence was simply a code name for capitulation.

Reagan came to power after the U.S. defeat in Vietnam. A powerful antiwar movement at home opposed American overseas military intervention. Henry Kissinger's attempt to replace it by a proxy war in Angola had been an ignominious failure. But Reagan was determined to turn the alliance with apartheid South Africa into a strategic one: "constructive engagement." He provided South Africa with a decade-long political umbrella to create from scratch Africa's first genuine terrorist movement (Resistência Nacional Moçambicana [RENAMO] in Mozambique) and another movement that vacillated between terror and political organization (União Nacional para a Independência Total de Angola [UNITA] in Angola) and then duplicated that project in Nicaragua (the Contras). The "great communicator" claimed that terror—specifically referring to

UNITA in Angola, the Contras in Nicaragua, and the Mujahideen in Afghanistan—was the spread of the "democratic revolution" and in 1985 went so far as to herald the leaders of the Contras and the Mujahideen as the "moral equivalents of America's Founding Fathers."

The Afghan jihad was a hothouse where the protagonists driving the present war on terror—the neocons and the jihadis—matured ideologically and politically. In their reformulation of Islam as resting on one pillar (jihad), of jihad as mainly military, and of military jihad as no longer about a community's self-defense but about the righteous assertion of an individual, jihadi Islam must be understood as a form of born-again Islam, a worldly counterpart to contemporary born-again Christianity and born-again Judaism.

Debate Five: The Search for Moderate Muslims or Defining Friend and Enemy in Contemporary America

I found the discussion on this question at times more revealing as a source of information on the participants in the debate than on Muslims, whether moderate or not. Is the defining characteristic of a moderate Muslim nonviolence, or is it openness to the idea of evolutionary change? Should we think of "moderation" and "extremism" as representing virtue and vice or in context, as, indeed, John F. Kennedy did in his inaugural address? Is it true that extremists are best thought of as spoiled grown-up children who cry not because of a particular grievance but because they want attention? Is the search for moderates, as one participant jokes, simply a search for those who are "like us"? Or, as another claims, does it come from an interest born more of policing than of intellectual instincts?

I am reminded of a book by Harvard literary theorist Werner Sollors: *Beyond Ethnicity: Consent and Descent in American Culture* (New York: Oxford University Press, 1986). In a fascinating chapter on post–Civil War America, Sollors discusses how American literature celebrated the "good" (read: moderate) Indian—young Indians who were willing to defy the patriarchal authority of parents and chiefs in the name of romantic love, even willing to commit suicide—precisely when the American polity was getting ready to carry out a massive ethnic cleansing exercise: the Indian Removals of the nineteenth century.

History teaches us that any search—whether it is the search for the "good Jew," the "good African American" or the "good African," or indeed "the noble savage"—that claims to divide a people between "good" and "bad," "moderate" and "extremist," must ring a warning bell.

DEBATE SIX: THE PRECONDITIONS OF REFORM

How are Muslim-majority societies to reform? Some worry about the absence of internal freedom and of Muslim intellectuals with the capacity for original thinking. Others worry about external pressures likely to generate a closed-door mentality: the Muslim World is under siege, and the war on terror demands nothing less than capitulation as the seal of recognition of a "good" or "moderate" Muslim. Under such circumstances, is it not likely that every self-respecting Muslim will be moved to fight under the banner of Islam, radical or not, if only out of self-respect?

Muslims do not just live in Muslim-majority societies; more and more live in Muslim-minority societies. Both, however, are likely to reach similar conclusions from day-to-day political experiences. Like all minorities, Muslim minorities too will learn to distinguish between religious and political community, for without this distinction they will win neither the right of belief nor the rights of a citizen. The same lesson is also relevant for Muslim majorities. Half a century after the end of colonialism, many recognize that the politicization of the religious community will inflame every religious difference as political: not only between Sunni and Shia but also between sects (for example, Ahmadiyya, Isma'ili, the Twelvers), not only between majority and minority but also inside the majority. With different schools of law inside Sunni Islam, whose interpretation of the Shariah is to be enforced by the power of the state (rather than observed voluntarily)?

Some argue that the real difference between those with a capacity to reform and those without is their attitude to ijtihad and jihad. One participant warns that ijtihad has been raised to a strategic slogan by official America and stands for a political agenda. Others warn of two notions of ijtihad—one so narrow and technical as to leave it to experts and deprive it of any democratic content, and the other so loose as to be without any sense of limits and so lend itself to a project that aims to liquidate Islam in the name of Islam. A reflection on the discussion suggests the need to think of a third and middle possibility, which recognizes the right of ijtihad as belonging to all but residing within limits framed by "fundamentals."

But can we think of ijtihad as an antidote to jihad? The right to reform, in the final analysis, is a right that belongs to nonpolitical organizations that can establish meaningful autonomy as well as to political communities that can defend sovereignty. The end of the cold war has shown that it is precisely those societies that Jeanne Kirkpatrick labeled "totalitarian" (as opposed to "authoritarian") and said could not reform from within that have managed to do so. China, Russia, and other parts of the former Soviet Union are spectacular examples of this ongoing process. In contrast, North Korea is being put under the gun and asked to reform, with little chance of doing so. Turkey won the right to reform; Algeria was denied it, as was Iraq, in both cases at great human cost. We hope that the lesson has been learned and that others branded as part of that club—Iran and Syria—will be spared that terrible fate.

CONCLUSION

Half a century after Strauss and six years into the war on terror, Anne Norton (a former student from the Straussian circle at the University of Chicago) wrote a book called *Leo Strauss and the Politics of American Empire* (New Haven: Yale University Press, 2004), once again raising the question of whether America is a truly liberal society. Her focus is placed on those people who claim to be the intellectual heirs of Strauss and are using their newfound political influence to frame a new enemy and champion the building of a new American empire: "Once it was another set of Semites who could not be trusted, whose primary loyalties lay elsewhere, who needed to be given a clear message about what was expected of them.... Now it is the Muslims who are involved in shadowy global conspiracies, Muslims who have 'fellow travelers.' The old language of anti-Semitism has found another target" (p. 212).

In this context the study of Muslims is bound to turn into a veritable industry, for modern empires are given to investing substantial resources to study the enemy. But unlike the study of the former Soviet Union and contemporary China, both with meaningful sovereignty, the study of Islam and Muslim societies is likely to take place on both sides of the border. Official America will fund Islam-watchers on this side of the border as well as professional "good" Muslim NGOs on the other side. Both are likely to grow in a mutually sustaining relationship. Unfortunately, neither is likely to be the source of independent and original thinking.

Chapter 16

THE TRANSFORMATION OF A TURKISH ISLAMIC MOVEMENT

From Identity Politics to Policy

M. HAKAN YAVUZ

SOME SCHOLARS, such as Graham Fuller, tend to read the current experiment in Turkey as the successful political integration of an Islamic
movement into a democracy.[1] Several facts support such an interpretation.
Although the JDP (Justice and Development Party) leadership denies its
Islamic background and claims to be a conservative democratic party, it
did emerge out of the ashes of the Welfare Party and the Virtue Party,
which were closed down by the constitutional court on charges of being a
forum for and proponent of antisecular activities.[2] Moreover, the majority
of JDP's deputies are observant Muslims in their daily lives. For instance,
their spouses continue to wear headscarves, which are banned in public
offices, state ceremonies, and universities because they are regarded as a
threat to Turkey's secular character. The religious observance of JDP's
members poses several questions. Is the JDP an Islamic party? Is it possible
for an ex-Islamic movement to become non-Islamic or un-Islamic? Is the
commitment of the JDP's members to religious values in their personal
life sufficient to label the party Islamic? When does a movement or a party
become or cease to be Islamic? Even if the party administration denies any
connection with political Islam, can we still consider the party Islamic?

Alternatively, we may argue that JDP's denial of being an Islamic party
is simply a compromise between the state and the JDP. The party, as the
argument goes, is free to govern the country as long as it stays within Turkey's strictly proscribed constitutional framework and ignores many of its
conservative constituency's religious demands. This alternative interpretation further complicates the issue and raises the following question: rather

than being the success story of an Islamic movement that has adapted to a democratic and secular environment, is the JDP an example of the Turkish system's ability to transform and domesticate political Islam to the extent that it denies its Islamism and even its Islamic roots?

Despite popular arguments to the contrary, it is very problematic to use Turkey as a model for Islamic democracy. Moreover, the Turkish experiment cannot be re-created in other Muslim countries, for several unique features (also mentioned by Ariel Cohen) differentiate Turkey from other Muslim countries. At the core of the Turkish experiment are four formative factors that dominate its political landscape.[3] First, Turkey has a very powerful tradition and history of a state structure and a state-centric political culture in comparison with other Muslim countries. Historically, the Ottoman imperial system was not in conflict with Islam; rather, Islam was subordinated to the state's interests.[4]

Second, Turkey has no legacy of colonialism or confrontation with the West. Consequently, Turkish political thought (secular or Islamic) was never suffused with anti-European ideas;[5] it always remained open to diverse ideas and lifestyles.

Third, the Turkish military was the founding institution of the republic and has a doctrine and mission for modernizing and secularizing Turkey. It has never collaborated with outside forces and did not allow any ideological clique to hijack its project. The military remains a more prestigious and respected institution than any religious organization.

Fourth, Turkey is not a rentier economy but rather a tax-based market economy with a growing middle class. Islam has been the transmission belt between state and nation, and the diversified economy has provided the necessary context for the pluralization of Islamic movements. The rigid interpretation of secularism failed to take into account that Turks are religious beings and that Islamic mores are the building blocks of their personal evolution and everyday life. In order to live a purposeful life in the Turkish context, one needs to have a cognitive map rooted in Turko-Islamic civilization. John Esposito aptly argues that each country has its own democratization process and that there is no single pattern for the relationship between political culture and democracy. Graham Fuller's reading of Erdogan as a "vital figure in the global evolution of political Islam" is rather naïve. Ruling under the shadow of military interventions and in the context of Turkey's political and cultural particularities, Erdogan represents only the transformation of a Turkish Islamic movement and certainly not the imagined "global political Islam."

Moreover, Turkey itself has not persuasively solved significant problems in regard to integrating political Islam into its system by accommodating it; rather, it has used extrajudicial means to transform political Islam to the point that the movement seeks refuge in denying its past and reacting very negatively when it is called "Islamic" or "Muslim." As such, the JDP refuses to define itself as an Islamic or Muslim party.

If an Islamic political movement actively opposes the articulation of arguments on the basis of Islamic values, I would argue that it is no longer Islamic. A movement is Islamic to the extent that it makes political claims and seeks legitimacy on Islamic grounds. In the case of Turkey, we see such a process—the process of post-Islamism or the shift from the politics of identity to the politics of services (*hizmet partisi*). We see the realization/materialization of liberal politics in Turkey in the sense that political movements are not engaged in the politics of identity, which tend to be conflict-ridden and confrontational, but rather in the politics of services, based on compromise and cooperation. As a result, a new social and political contract is evolving, premised on neoliberal economic and political values. This can be seen as the normalization of Turkish politics, because it hints at the country's positive integration into many of the macrotrends taking place on a global scale. The JDP, being the product of these transformations, is not a party of identity but rather a party that strives to provide better services. It does not develop or articulate any claims on the basis of Islam or other sources of identity but acts as an agent of the country's integration into neoliberal economic and political spaces.

Going back to our main question, when and under what conditions a movement ceases to be Islamic, I would argue that this occurs if it abstains from articulating policies based on Islamic identity and employs public reason instead of using Islamic justifications. Based on the JDP's actions, it is possible to conclude that the Islamic political movement has helped to consolidate democracy by offering Turkey's marginalized groups an alternative avenue for political participation. Yet this positive role is very much an outcome of expanding opportunity spaces and restraining the military-legal institutions. In large part, this became possible through the actions and trend-setting role played by a new and rising Anatolian bourgeoisie, whose members have refused to support confrontational policies. This democratic bargaining between the state and the JDP forced the latter to give up any search for governmental "hegemony" and to accept European Union (EU)–oriented democratic norms. Turkey's Islamic groups, more than the secularists, reluctantly supported this new democratic bargain because they intrinsically understood that it was the only way for them to come to power.

These EU norms helped to domesticate and force not only the state but also the antisystemic actors to change their perspectives and strategies and to adopt such norms as the point of reference to create a new social contract. When the EU gives a possible accession date, it is not very clear how the JDP will react. Although some of its members are in the process of inventing some sort of post-EU platform, other broad-based programs that would appeal to the JDP's past supporters have yet to be articulated. There is still a major chance for Turkish voters to return to the identity-based parties of the past, having used the JDP as a streetcar to reach their desired destination (namely, EU membership), and to cleanse the political landscape of corrupt politicians. I believe that this is the biggest question facing Turkish politics in the near future. In other words, has politics in Turkey really shifted from the politics of identity to the politics of issues/services, or is the case of the JDP simply a temporary development if not an anomaly?

THE SOURCE OF THE SILENT REVOLUTION: THE NEW BOURGEOISIE

The Turkish case challenges two dominant Orientalist theses: that Islam and democracy as well as capitalism and Islam are incompatible. In the case of Turkey, we see the evolution of an Islam that is both entrepreneurial and capitalist-oriented. The rise of a Muslim bourgeoisie is a challenge to the Weberian reading of the relationship between Islam and capitalism as one of incompatibility and antagonism. By "Muslim entrepreneurs," I mean those pious individuals who identify Islam as their identity and formulate their everyday cognitive map by using Islamic ideas and history to vernacularize (Islamicize) modern economic relations that promote market forces and cherish the neoliberal project.

Political Islam is most often depicted as the enemy of the West and the Western values of capitalism, democracy, human rights, and modernity. Daniel Lerner's image of "Mecca or Mechanization" has been replaced by Benjamin Barber's "Jihad vs. McWorld." The case of Turkey can be used to challenge and question this dichotomous mode of thinking: it not only indicates the compatibility between Islam and democracy, as well as between Islam and capitalism, but also shows how new waves of globalization have opened new spaces for the evolution and consolidation of Islamic economic actors.

The Islamic movement in Turkey, which is led by a counterelite with a counterproject, is progressive in ways that challenge the state ideology (Kemalism) and the secular bloc (military-bureaucracy-capitalist) and also critique "traditional/folk" Islamic ways of doing and thinking. The neoliberal project produced new Islamic actors who, in turn, shaped Islamic discourse and practices. The market's expansion, the increasing role of the middle class, and a strengthened civil society have had a profound impact on Islamic actors and their identities.

To understand the JDP's origins and policies, we have to explore not only the sociopolitical context of the new Muslim actors (the Muslim bourgeoisie) but also its identity, politics, and relationship with Islamic political groups. It is very important to study the role of the Islamic bourgeoisie, because it provides the financial means to develop the Islamic movement through its charities, television stations, radios, and newspapers and, as such, has boosted its social status.

Who are these actors? What are their identity and politics? How do they shape the JDP's orientation? What is the role of the Muslim bourgeoisie in the fragmentation, and even the end, of Islamism? The Islamic movement is not shaped by the shantytowns surrounding large cities in Turkey, but rather by rising social groups in terms of wealth and education. These are the groups, especially the Muslim bourgeoisie, that are fueling the locomotive of Islamization regarding consumer patterns and that are the vanguard of Turkey's recent democratization.

The Muslim bourgeoisie evolved out of the state's neoliberal economic policies, which, by deregulating and opening the Turkish economy, created conducive economic conditions and emerging transnational financial networks. Its members have also benefited from the local governments of the Welfare Party, especially after 1994. This new actor is both a cause and an outcome of the neoliberal economic policies of Turgut Özal, the former reformist prime minister and president, who died in 1993. The symbiotic relationship between the state and the large Istanbul-based capitalists had rested on both parties' agreement over secularism and Kemalism. The emergence of an Anatolian-based Muslim bourgeoisie ran counter to the existing economic and cultural alliance between the state and the Istanbul-based capitalists.

These Muslim entrepreneurs consist mostly of first-generation college graduates of an Anatolian-based petty bourgeoisie whose members benefited from Özal's neoliberal economic policies, which increased their social mobility and thus enabled them to establish their own medium-sized and small firms. They are the first generation of an urbanizing economic elite that continues to maintain strong ties with Anatolia's provincial towns and villages. Most of them were born and raised there and settled in the big cities only after graduating from college. They were first introduced to Islamic values in their provincial towns and villages and later spent several years in university dormitories, mostly run by Nurcu or Naksibendi Sufi orders. In addition, they objectified Islam as an alternative project and became conscious Muslims with a clear and concise notion of what constituted an Islamic identity. Thus a closer study indicates that most of the members of MÜSIAD (the Association of Independent Industrialists and Businessmen), a conscious Muslim business association, appear to have come from a conservative Muslim social environment with a history of antiestablishment discontent. They were—and still are—critical of state subsidies for the Istanbul-based business class and have always been disgruntled with Turkey's history of state/big business connections.

The state mostly excluded and marginalized this petty bourgeoisie by following import-substitution policies and, from the foundation of the Turkish Republic onward, always favoring a secular-oriented big city–based bourgeoisie as the carrier of its modernization projects and purveyor of its prescribed lifestyles. Most members of this new urbanizing economic elite became involved in the growing textile and construction trade. Eventually services, transportation, and tourism became important fields of activity. Most of these small and medium-sized firms are family owned and maintain family structures with conservative religious values. In other words, even though members of this new economic elite all come from a traditional petty-bourgeois background and a culturally marginalized milieu, they used education and the new economic and political conditions of the post-1980s to develop entrepreneurial and organizational skills so that they could reposition themselves as Anatolia's new economic actors in order to modernize their cities and lifestyles through Islamization.

These new actors identified the state's interventionist policies and its ties to big business as being responsible for Turkey's uneven economic development and socioeconomic problems as well as for excluding a large sector of the petty bourgeoisie. They mobilized their Islamic identity, which the Kemalist elite had marginalized and identified as the cause of Turkey's backwardness, to challenge state policies and form a new organization to articulate their policies. In other words, Islamic identity was not a cause but rather was used as the lubricant to prime the workings of market forces and as an instrument for carving out their share in the market.

The transformative history of MÜSIAD is the history of this new urbanizing economic elite, which is steeped in Islamic ethics and networks.

Thus entrepreneurial Islam is the outcome of this new elite, which critiques the Istanbul-based secularist elite and the traditional Islamic conception of *isnaf* (small merchants).

The expansion of economic opportunity not only facilitated the evolution of more moderate political forces but also enhanced civil society and private education. These autonomous economic groups supported a number of cultural projects, along with new television stations, radio channels, and magazines.

In conclusion, the JDP defines itself as being outside of political Islam. It constantly reminds itself of what it is not: an Islamic party. But its repressed identity occasionally reemerges. Inevitably, the party's identity is shaped both by what it wants to forget and by what it wants to become. It reflects a conflict between Islamism and the new rubric of "conservative democracy," the term used by party leaders to demonstrate that they are not Islamic. The party has particularly exploited the EU membership project to demonstrate that it is not Islamic in either domestic or foreign policy. Conforming to the Copenhagen criteria is an aspect of this identity building.

NOTES

1. Graham E. Fuller, "Turkey's Strategic Model: Myths and Realities," *Washington Quarterly* 27, no. 3 (Summer 2004): 51–64. Daniel Pipes also argued: "The Justice and Development Party in Turkey is very different from the Taliban in its means, but not so different in its ends. If the party gained full control over Turkey, it could be as dangerous as the Taliban were in Afghanistan" (Washington Institute, *Policy Watch* 746, April 10, 2003, at http://www.washingtoninstitute.org/templateC05.php?CID=1624).

2. M. Hakan Yavuz, *Islamic Political Identity in Turkey* (New York: Oxford University Press, 2003).

3. Jenny B. White, *Islamist Mobilization in Turkey: A Study in Vernacular Politics* (Seattle: University of Washington Press, 2003); M. Hakan Yavuz, *Islamic Political Identity* (London: Oxford University Press, 2003); Nilufer Göle, *The Forbidden Modern: Civilization and Veiling* (Ann Arbor: University of Michigan Press, 1999).

4. Carter Vaughn Findley, *The Turks in World History* (New York: Oxford University Press, 2004).

5. M. Hakan Yavuz, "Is There a Turkish Islam?" *Journal of Muslim Minority Affairs* 24, no. 4 (October 2004): 213–32.

Chapter 17

REFLECTIONS ON THE DEBATE

TAHA JABIR AL-ALWANI

I HAVE REVIEWED all of the answers of my respected colleagues and find that I agree with most of their points. Therefore, in my comments, I would like to focus on some points that researchers should concentrate on in order to enrich our understanding and comprehension of the Muslim community in the United States. Doing so will help engender good and strong relations among the different groups in American society.

ON MODERATE MUSLIMS

Before I explain the term "moderate Muslim," I would like to indicate that American officials have trouble working with moderate Muslims because they see moderates as pragmatists who will change their positions based on their interests and use religion or sacred symbols to gain followers and support. True moderates use certain aspects of religion for their political interests and in this way become more intimidating to the fundamentalist or Islamist policymakers who do not hide their right-wing extremism and desire to hold onto their past culture. Such moderates, who are political pragmatists but theological lightweights, are easy to work with and more understandable. But their understanding of Islam is naïve and composed of stagnant interpretations.

These moderate Muslims accept many or all of the most important Western values related to politics, economics, education, and practical life. This puts them in a better position to understand the Western mind, how it thinks, and how to interact with it based on its own methodologies. Extremist Muslims allow no change in their culture, view history as passive, and consider any changes in life quantitative, not qualitative. Thus they believe that they can resurrect history and bring back the earlier Islamic centuries, especially the time of the Companions, by repeating their paths, methodologies, and tools. Such attitudes make them out-of-touch with modern realities in the Westerners' opinion, however, and they are therefore easily isolated.

A Muslim, if he or she wants to remain Muslim, cannot deny or ignore certain pillars of belief, such as the five pillars of Islam, jihad, and encouraging what is right and forbidding what is wrong. Thus it is incorrect to say that moderate Muslims do not believe that jihad is one of Islam's pillars. Moderate Muslims see jihad in its complete and objective meaning, however, within a framework of self-purification, family, society, the larger human family, the environment, and the earth. In contrast, the "others" (conservatives) see jihad as limited to the jihad of the sword and divide it into offensive war (*jihad talab*) and defensive war (*jihad dafʿa*).

On Turkey

Turkey is a special case. Ever since it abolished the khilafah in March 1924, it has continued to swing between Kemalist secularism, which is openly hostile to religion, and Islam, which has sought to protect itself and keep what it can of Islamic identity alive. Turkish secularists moved away from Islam because they thought that for many centuries it had made "Muslim" rulers responsible for protecting the Ottoman people, whose only relation to the "family of Osman" was Islam. Therefore, they sought to put a complete divider between these secularists and Islam so that they could take Turkey back to its pre-Islamic paganism (*wathaniyah*) and realize their dream of joining Europe. Nonsecular Turks, however, consider belonging to Islam and Turkey's leadership of the Muslims to be important elements of their nation's glory. Moreover, Islam gave the Turks prestige and enabled the Ottoman Empire to become a superpower that gradually controlled land in the heart of Europe and expanded to Asia and Africa.

These nonsecularists believe that a return to Islam will give Turkey a chance once again to lead the Islamic world, resume its leadership position, and flourish. The secular Kemalists and the religious Turks agree on one issue: the glory of Turkey and the Turks and how to revive it. The Turkish mind cannot rid itself of the pressure of Islamic memories. Those who review the Turkish situation have to consider the historical background, especially the last two centuries (namely, the eighteenth and nineteenth) of the Ottoman Empire's existence. Therefore, it is hard to generalize the Islamic Turkish political model, which is modern, and apply it to other Muslim countries that do not share the same grand and ancient history. In addition, the Iranian Shahinshah (emperor) model and that of the post-Khomeini era cannot be generalized to the rest of the Muslim countries. Careful researchers need to focus on these matters before they introduce a model that cannot be applied throughout the Islamic world.

ON IJTIHAD

One of the participants refers to the myth that ijtihad was alive only among Shia scholars. In reality, the Shia refused to emulate (*taqlid*) dead scholars and called upon their community to follow live scholars. In modern times, both Shia and Sunnis have engaged in a lot of practical ijtihad. For example, Muhammad Abduh, Rashid Rida, and those who belonged to their school (for example, Ahmad Mustafa al-Muraghi and Mahmud Shaltut), and the heads of al-Azhar, Abu Zahra', and others all recorded their ijtihad concerning modern issues. And what about Sunni fiqhi fatwas on banking, contracts, redefining the meaning of riba (usury), and exempting mortgages on houses and cars? All of these are *ijtihadat*. Sunni, Shia, 'Ibadi, and Zaydi ulama participated in devising them. So if this is what is meant by ijtihad, then ijtihad did not stop, either realistically or practically, just because some people called for the door to be closed. This is yet another issue that needs to be researched and analyzed in a way that goes beyond just repeating what earlier writers have said when discussing the history of Islamic law.

THE "WRITING" OF THE QUR'AN

I have a reservation about using *kutiba* (written) in such cases as "the Qur'an was written." No one deserves to be called a Muslim unless he or she believes that the Qur'an was revealed by Allah to his Prophet Muhammad in one of the three ways of revelation mentioned in Qur'an 42:51. Everything that we say concerning the Qur'an also applies to the Torah, the Injil, and the Zabur, for God revealed all of these books to humanity through His prophets. If Allah had meant *allafa* (publish) or *uliffa* (it was prepared), then He would have used those words. In addition, the Sunnah was collected in 99 AH and written down. Muslims believe that the Qur'an is not limited by time and that the absolute is not influenced by the disagreement of the interpreters, which are based upon when they lived and the degree of their knowledge. Even if an interpretation changes, the absolute essence and subject of its text does not change. How the Qur'an is understood and absorbed in regard to the interpretational development of its meaning was discussed by specialists in the sciences of the foundations of fiqh (*usul al-fiqh*). Therefore, we do not accept that the Qur'an was written; such ideas reflect the researcher's ignorance.

On Ideology

Globalization has proved that no ideology can control the whole world. As the last two centuries have shown, Christianity cannot overcome other religions, especially Islam and Judaism, and neither can Islam defeat Christianity and Judaism. Humanity has finally managed to discover this truth. As a result, those who follow current events cannot help but believe that humanity needs to review such things as the ideological roots of religions, their interpretations, and how their followers understand their particular religions.

Therefore, the only choice is to go back to the core and absolute ethics on which people do not differ, even if they take different routes to prove and interpret them. These shared ethics are the only real guarantee to which people should refer and upon which people can build a strong relationship among the extended human family, which descends from one father and one mother and which makes the whole earth its home—a home that should be safe from any destruction and conflict. These shared ethics come from truth, the good, beauty, human unity, the unity of creation, equality among people, the necessity of freedom for men and women, and the necessity of justice to organize their lives.

If these shared ethics could be adopted and presented to humanity so that all people could understand and implement them in their lives, then humanity would adopt them. That is why ideologues are asked to use their ideologies in ways that support these ethics and convince other people to adhere to them. Then opportunities for understanding among people would arise, religious thought would become equal to worldly (*al-maniyah*) thought, and humanity would reach ever-higher levels of global progress instead of experiencing disagreement and conflict. Therefore, reformers, philosophers, and intellectuals should look into these common ethics, shed light on them, build awareness about them, and avoid opposing them, undermining their importance, or ignoring them by forcing other ideologies into conflict with them. In addition, these shared ethics would put everyone on the same level in every aspect and then produce effective tools for building the necessary common ground.

On the Presence of Islam in the West

This presence is normal and should not be classified as "dangerous" or "not dangerous." It is the result of many factors, the most important of which are the global nature of Western civilization and the extraordinary infrastructures and communication methods that its people have produced in their quest for change and self-improvement. All of this has made contemporary men and women very mobile, for it enables them to view growth and material prosperity as more important than their connection with the homeland, unlike, for example, agricultural societies, where people would rather die than leave their homeland.

Muslims migrated to the West for several reasons. Chief among them are the failures of their own societies and the failure of the modernization models adopted by their home countries. Muslims left their homes in search of a better life in Europe and the United States. Once in the West, probably less than 5 percent of them rebuilt their Islamic identity. In the first stage, they reminded themselves and their families that they already had an identity and belonged to something and that Islam was an important pillar of their identity. They helped each other build a mosque and then a school to prevent the remnants of their former identity from draining away. When they felt that they had adequately protected this identity and that they could maintain it and pass it along, they started to introduce themselves to their neighbors as being their equal, for Muslims are not lower in status than other Americans. Thus religious Muslims moved from protecting their essence to building relationships. Along the way, some Christians converted to Islam for a wide variety of reasons. If we compare the number of these converts with those of Muslim young people who have abandoned Islam, however, especially those whose lives are identical to those of their non-Muslim American and European peers, the picture is not very good. In addition, many Muslims continue to convert to Christianity.

Due to the "scary" idea that Islam is spreading quickly, such televangelists as Jimmy Swaggart, Pat Robertson, and the late Jerry Falwell continue to spread fear and anxiety so that their followers will donate more money. In addition to making them feel threatened, these evangelists find other ways to push their followers to be more religiously loyal and strengthen their attachment to the church. If we are to answer this challenge, our scholars need to undertake detailed academic studies that go beyond the feelings and pretensions of such people. Unfortunately, the American corporate media have adopted these negative orientations.

Another factor that makes Americans scared of Islam and Muslims is the ongoing revival of the memory of the Crusades and all of its legacy and literature, transformed into stories, novels, and plays. Thousands of such tropes, based on the *Arabian Nights* as well as literature related to the

Crusades and European colonialism in the Muslim World, are still found in Western markets. These show the worst aspects of the way in which the Muslims distorted Islam and are now being used to remind Westerners to feel uncomfortable with the Muslim presence in their societies.

Finally, the United States and Europe could use the presence of Islam in their midst to build better relationships with the Islamic world, instead of spreading fear among their citizens. And Allah knows best. Muslims seek to build upon the above-mentioned shared morals. Moreover, their values are very close to those of the Founding Fathers, particularly in regard to family values and protecting the environment. Thus Muslims can help Americans rebuild their traditional core values. Before 9/11 the United States prided itself on being made up of different communities. But after that tragedy many people and organizations started to emphasize what they saw as the negative aspects of various communities, primarily the Muslim ones.

{V}

THE LAST WORD

Chapter 18

DEFINING A MODERATE

KAMRAN A. BOKHARI AND FARID SENZAI

PROLOGUE

AS WE HAVE SEEN, the debate about moderate Islam and Muslims is often heated and highly controversial, especially if we compare the positions of Ariel Cohen on one end of the spectrum with the views of Abid Ullah Jan on the other end. There are two reasons for this disconnect. First, many non-Muslims like Cohen have an implicit and more recently explicit desire to see the rise of moderates in the midst of what is seen as a global trend toward radicalism. In other words, they assume that both Islam and its adherents need to gravitate toward moderation because this is not an inherent feature of Muslims or their faith. On the flip side, many Muslims like Jan view this pressure as suspicious, intrusive, and often hostile. Moreover, the call for moderation is seen by Jan and many of his persuasion as part of a larger plan by the West to dilute their religion.

The sad news is that in recent years a disproportionate number of both Muslims and non-Muslims have been gravitating toward the two ends of this spectrum. It may be satisfying for many who like their heroes and villains portrayed in simple dichotomies to try to define Muslims similarly as either "good" or "bad." Thus, for instance, in Cohen's view Sheikh Kabbani falls in the "good" camp, while Tariq Ramadan falls in the "bad" camp. Yet this type of simplistic approach will not get us very far in understanding moderate Muslims or addressing the root causes of the hatred and violence projected against us. Neither view bodes well for efforts to build bridges or resolve the conflict. More importantly, these views are an incorrect assessment of reality and only further exacerbate the tension between the West and the Muslim World.

As the debate and now war over moderate Islam continues to recruit adherents, some elements from both sides now suggest that this is primarily a "battle of ideas." The September 14 remarks by President George W. Bush in an address to the 60th annual session of the United Nations General Assembly are noteworthy. In his presentation the president suggested that global terrorism could not be combated through military means alone. Instead, he stressed that the principal battle in this war is over ideas. Bush underscored that defeating transnational militant Islamist nonstate actors required a victory in this realm.

At first glance, the notion that this is in fact a "battle of ideas" may sound appealing, but it raises more questions than it answers: (1) What constitutes an ideational battle? (2) How can one successfully engage in an intellectual struggle? (3) Who are the participants in this new type of cold war? (4) What kind of arsenal do the belligerents bring to bear in this clash?

While the physical war continues between a U.S.-led coalition of states deploying their intelligence and military assets and jihadists affiliated with or inspired by the global militant Islamist al-Qaeda network, the intellectual confrontation remains an intra-Muslim affair, rather than one between Muslims and non-Muslims. Put differently, Westerners, or non-Muslims, are at best playing the role of catalysts in the ideological tussle between radical/militant Islamists and moderate Muslims. If extremist forces are to be defeated, it will be at the hands of authentic and legitimate Muslim actors, who are not tainted by accusations of being Western pawns.

In fact, the extremists are already trying to exploit the moderate Muslim/Western interface by painting those who are calling for moderation as a Western fifth column in the body of the ummah. The statements of al-Qaeda's chief in Iraq, Abu Musab al-Zarqawi, were a clear example of this. In an audiotaped communiqué ironically released on the same day that Bush articulated the "battle of ideas" concept, al-Zarqawi best characterized the cooperation between Washington and Iraq's majority Shia community as a "Crusader-Shiite alliance" against the country's Sunni population.

While Muslim states have remained allies of the United States against Muslim extremists ever since the September 11 attacks, such an alliance in the ideational combat zone not only is difficult to assemble but threatens to defeat the purpose of the conflict altogether. Put differently, material interests can bring together states who would otherwise be unlikely allies; however, securing such collaboration is next to impossible, given the involvement of conflicting ideas. It is no secret that while the vertical Muslim regimes remain firmly in the U.S. political camp for a variety of reasons (including self-interest), anti-Americanism runs rampant among the horizontal Muslim masses.

Here it is important to point out that this behavioral variance is not because Muslim peoples subscribe to radical and militant Islamist ideologies but because they disdain the idea of being subjugated by a foreign superpower. Therefore, the role that the United States or Europe can play in this "battle of ideas" is, at most, indirect encouragement of moderate Muslim voices. Essentially, it must allow the intra-Muslim debate to follow its own natural course.

Given that Islamist radicals are plagued by a poverty of thought, on a level playing field unencumbered by outside interference the extremists will be exposed to the Muslim masses, who are in search of ideas that not only are in keeping with their cultural values but also offer solutions to the political, social, and economic problems of everyday life. Most Muslims will recognize that at best the radicals represent a reactionary protest movement that does not offer prescriptions for the ills of the Muslim World and at worst they constitute a security threat to the ummah.

The radicals will not be able to compete, provided the moderates are not seen as advancing un-Islamic concepts and alien values. The radicals will only thrive as long as they can generate and sustain the perception that moderates are U.S. and Western lackeys and point to an umbilical cord between the two.

The Bush administration understands the stakes of the game, and Bush's comments at the U.N. General Assembly session explain his administration's efforts to engage in negotiations with a variety of moderate Islamist and Muslim actors from all across the Muslim World and within the United States. It is no coincidence that Karen Hughes, Bush's newly appointed undersecretary for public diplomacy and public affairs, spoke at the annual convention of the Islamic Society of North America— the country's largest mainstream Muslim organization—in Chicago over Labor Day weekend in 2005. Hughes had just returned from a tour of Egypt, Saudi Arabia, and Turkey, in what she described as a listening mission.

That said, a lot more will have to be done if extremism is to be contained, most of which will be done by Muslim actors alone. While the Muslim World appreciates moderation, it has yet to come to terms with what Islamic moderation is all about.

The attacks of September 11, 2001, were followed by an upsurge in the global discourse involving moderate Muslims and moderate Islam. This issue is further problematized not only because the West, led by the United States, is trying to seek out the moderates in the Islamic world but also because diverse groups in Muslim states as well claim to be the upholders of moderate Islam and hence claim to be moderate Muslims. What is interesting in all of this is not the Western *demand* for moderation but the Muslim *supply* of moderation.

DEFINING THE TERM

It is essential to acknowledge that the very notion of defining a "moderate Muslim" is a highly contested endeavor. As Graham Fuller accurately points out, "it all depends on what person you ask." The most appropriate method and our personal preference would be to allow Muslims to define themselves. Let the Muslims decide who is a "moderate" and who is not. After all, it is the same litmus test we use for people of other faiths.

For the sake of this discussion, however, if we are pushed to come up with a definition, then we need to set a minimum threshold. According to Fuller, a moderate Muslim is "one who shuns literalism and selectivism in the understanding of sacred texts." The problem with this definition is that all peoples—not just Muslims—to varying degrees engage in literalism and selectivism. For example, the consensus among Muslims that Islam forbids the consumption of alcohol is a type of literalism in that it is based on textual sources that have been declared not to be subject to variant interpretations. In other words, literalism as a concept is difficult to define. The problems of definition render its application even more problematic.

As for selectivism, people of all religious and ideological persuasions privilege certain historical figures and trends over others. Many even engage in the construction of false reverse historical continuums and push the idea that it has always been this way—meaning their preferred understanding.

A better qualification is accepting ijtihadic pluralism, because it is broad enough that Muslims from sundry ideological backgrounds can be deemed moderate so long as they are willing to accept that—while they consider their respective positions the most accurate—other Muslims can and will have understandings different from theirs. In turn, the notion of plurality in ijtihad allows for the development of the norm of tolerance. A moderate would reject the idea that any one group or individual has a monopoly on defining Islam and would seek to emphasize common ground with other faiths rather than accentuate the differences.

Furthermore, the word "moderate" is relative in two respects. First, when we refer to an individual, group, or state as being moderate, we mean that it is moderate in relation to other individuals, groups, or states from the common cultural background. The Muslim Brotherhood in the Arab Middle East is considered a moderate Islamist group compared to al-Qaeda. Iran's Islamic republic is moderate when compared to Afghanistan under the Taliban Emirate. Second, the use of the term "moderate" presupposes a benchmark to gauge the deviation or conformity of an individual, group, or state. This raises the question of what criterion can be used to classify individuals, groups, and states as moderate. The search for an answer to this question, we believe, must commence with a consideration of the various grammatical usages of this expression.

According to the Merriam-Webster dictionary, the word "moderate" can be used in three grammatical forms: as an adjective, as a verb, and as a noun. When used as a noun, it refers to the one who bears moderate views or who is affiliated with a group pursuing a moderate approach or agenda. As a verb, "to moderate" means to lower the concentration or excessiveness of something. It could also mean to become less aggressive, harsh, or intense. Finally, as an adjective, "moderate" means shunning extreme behavior or expression. In other words, it symbolizes the qualities of the one who observes equitable limits. To be a moderate in this sense could be understood as tending toward the center as opposed to the periphery. "Moderate" has also been used to typify political or social beliefs that are not of a radical nature.

Having established the lexical boundaries of the term "moderate," let us now take a look at the nature of those in the Muslim World who claim to be moderates. It has actually become somewhat fashionable among Muslims these days to refer to oneself or one's ilk as being moderate. At least four different types of Muslims advance themselves as the adherents of moderate Islam. Among this medley of those who claim to be the champions of moderate Islam are moderate Islamists, traditional Muslims, liberal Muslims, and certain regimes in the Muslim World.

Moderate Islamists claim the mantle of moderate Islam in a bid to distinguish themselves from the radical and militant types. Traditional Muslims who are different from the moderate Islamists in that they do not advance a particular political ideology based on Islam are quick to point out that they have always constituted the majority of Muslims historically. They emphasize that they gained their status as the historical main-stream of Islam by refraining from adopting any immoderate tendencies to advance their cause. Most practicing Muslims (a great many of whom perhaps identify with the Sufi strand of Islam) fall in this category. Liberal Muslims represent the third group: those who might adhere to a certain minimalist degree of personal religious commitment but for the most part have embraced secularity in the public realm. This category, due to its privileged status as being equipped with Western education, seeks to claim exclusive leadership over moderate Islam for the purposes of securing its rather elitist standing in the Muslim countries.

These three categories concern nonstate actors, but states are also quite active in this quest to appear moderate. It is interesting to note that a generation ago some of these states strongly promoted Islam as a means to legitimize their raison d'être. In fact, in this process such regimes allied themselves with certain radical tendencies, which at that time were con-fined to the fringes of society. Patronage from states had a huge strengthen-ing effect on these marginal entities. It is quite ironic that certain regimes that were hitherto nurturing militant Islamists to consolidate their hold on power are now threatened by their own protégés. Some of these regimes in the Muslim World, who have issued a clarion call for moderation in the wake of September 11, 2001, constitute the fourth category of Muslims ad-vancing themselves as the torchbearers of moderate Islam. These include Pakistan, Saudi Arabia, Iran, Malaysia, Turkey, Egypt, and others.

In Search of Authenticity

Contemporary Islamic resurgence, whose roots can be traced back to the late nineteenth century, is a movement in search of a modern but Islami-cally authentic response to the dominance of Western civilization. From this tendency emerged the ideology of Islamism, which eventually became hyperfactionalized. The quest for authenticity became an intra-Islamist af-fair as much as it was an intra-Muslim debate. As it stands today, Islamists to varying degrees view moderation as a function of secularism. Islamists see a direct correlation between calls for moderation and secularism. They fear that any attempts at the development of a moderate discourse on Islam will lead to the secularization and hence dilution of Islam.

Most fascinating is the intra-Islamist debate, in which different types of Islamists, in an effort to claim authenticity for their particular dis-course, refer to their rival trends as being secular. If we begin with the jiha-dists, they claim that all other types of Islamists (including their nonjihadi neo-Salafist co-ideologues) exhibit secularist inclinations. Moving away from this extreme, we find the Hizb al-Tahrir types, arguing that they themselves are not Islamists who have fallen prey to secularism and that they too condemn such Islamists. From the point of view of Hizb al-Tahrir, al-Muhajiroun, Tanzeem-i-Islami, and similar groups, the Muslim Brotherhood types are Islamists gone secular. The Muslim Brotherhood also refutes such allegations, however, and points to the non-Islamist Muslims as being the true secularists in the Muslim World. As we move along the Islamist political spectrum from the extreme of the jihadists to the Muslim Brotherhood types, we find an interesting pattern: a decreasing tendency toward literal interpretation of the texts.

At the heart of all this is the desire of Islamists for authenticity and legitimacy. Generally speaking, Islamists do not like labels such as moderate, radical, and militant as identification markers because they see this as an attempt by the West to create dissension among the ranks of the ummah, to dilute Islam, and to target Muslims for the purposes of political persecution. While some or even all of this may be true to some degree, the problem involves the confusion between normative principles and empirical realities among many Islamists. They need to appreciate the difference between Islamic principles and their operationalization in real life. In other words, Muslims adopt moderate, radical, and militant means to promote Islam.

Epilogue

The Muslim World has been under a lot of external ideological pressure to reform Islamic thought ever since a group of militant Islamists ploughed passenger planes into the twin towers of the World Trade Center. This in turn has generated intense internal competition in regard to the actual locus of moderate Muslims and the race to define moderate Islam. Variant types of Muslims are scrambling to appropriate this new space known as moderate Islam. Regardless of how we define moderate Islam, we need to recognize the upper and lower limits of this space.

It is essential to define the lower limit strictly and the upper limit loosely. Put differently, we have an acute need to underscore that moderate Islam is about respecting the plurality of ijtihad and rejecting violence as a means of capturing the political center-stage in the Muslim World. Shunning the use of force to promote a particularistic political agenda should be the minimum requirement to qualify as a moderate Muslim. This does not mean abandoning the right to self-defense and just war, but this right must be exercised at least in accordance with one fundamental principle.

Muslim groups *must not* target noncombatants and their civilian property, for this is the very essence of terrorism.

What is intriguing in this regard is that those who would otherwise argue for a literalist interpretation of the texts engage in twisted logic when they wish to justify their use of violence. Normally we would see such groups tirelessly elevating revelation over reason, but they succumb to the temptation of reason (albeit circular) to legitimize their modus operandi. As for the threshold of moderate Islam, it should be left sufficiently wide and open to allow for healthy exchange of ideas and free intellectual competition. This, we humbly submit, should be the criterion to identify moderate Muslims, lest this phrase end up being yet another exclusivist label.

Chapter 19

ACCOMMODATING "MODERATION"

A Return to Authenticity
or Recourse to Heresy?

ASMA AFSARUDDIN

THE ENGAGING AND PROVOCATIVE ESSAYS assembled in this volume address a number of timely and pertinent questions related to definitions of "moderate Muslims," the future of political Islam, the role of ijtihad in a possible "reformation" of Islam, and Islam and its place in the West. The commentators were astutely chosen to represent a broad spectrum of views, so that one may honestly say that this book represents a fair and highly representative sampling of responses to the broad questions posed. John Esposito, Graham Fuller, and Muqtedar Khan are three prominent interlocutors representing the more academic, mainstream, and well-informed points of view. Their complementary responses reflect nuanced, reflective positions on many of these critical issues, born of a long-standing familiarity with Muslims and the Muslim World and based on careful scholarship regarding many of the issues. Their remarks show a perceptive analysis of the historical and sociopolitical factors contributing to the rise of political Islam and its appeal and the role that so-called moderate Muslims and their hermeneutic enterprise can play in counteracting its potential stranglehold.

Additional commentaries by Feisal Abdul Rauf, Ali A. Mazrui, Louay Safi, Mahmood Mamdani, M. Hakan Yavuz, and Taha Jabir al-Alwani provide valuable, apposite insights into the debates on moderate Islam, Islamic political identity, pluralism, the "clash of civilizations," the role of Western Muslims, and the scope of ijtihad, particularly in Qur'anic hermeneutics.

Two respondents merit special comment. Ariel Cohen represents a rather hardline right-wing and unabashedly chauvinistic (America right or wrong) point of view, preferring to sweep under the rug the consequences of wrong-headed U.S. foreign policy measures over the years in regard to the Middle East. Such views need to be represented, however, because they are common in influential policy circles and may even be considered fairly mainstream in contemporary America. Cohen is, of course, not a Middle Eastern specialist or a scholar of Islam. That is pretty evident from some of his more thoughtless and egregious generalizations about Islam and Muslims. His identification of Tariq Ramadan as an Islamist supporter of the Muslim Brotherhood shows how far afield he is. Cohen has a doctoral degree—an impressive academic credential. Coupled with his impassioned, knee-jerk responses, particularly in the second round of rebuttals, this proves the following case: many otherwise highly educated Americans continue to hold simplistic and frighteningly uninformed, monochromatic, and essentialist views of Arabs and Muslims. Shocking though they may seem to the specialist, such views have long been a staple in the State Department and in other policymaking circles. These perspectives have colored and continue to color the positions of many in the media and the academy as well—hence the need to have such views represented in this conversation.

On the seemingly opposite end of the spectrum, Abid Ullah Jan represents views tinged by a near-complete distrust and suspicion of the West and its presumed total hegemony. While he is to the left in such views, he also swings effortlessly to the right in his undisguised contempt for the "moderate" Muslim, who, he assumes, has compromised his or her religious heritage in order to appease the West. Some self-styled, professional "moderate" Muslims today indeed deserve much of this contempt, but his disdain extends to all those Muslims who would not subscribe to the full panoply of his opinions. Jan also displays a "fundamentalist" adherence to political Islam in his vision of a revived khilafah (caliphate), the precursor to a just world order and an Islamic utopia. His impassioned views, however, represent an important articulation of an alternative world order imagined by a considerable number of Muslims in reaction to the real and perceived political injustices inflicted upon their communities by various Western governments over time. Jan's invocation of the Islamist utopian enterprise of re-creating an assumed pristine Islamic state is an issue that has to be energetically reckoned with by moderate and modernist Muslims. Juxtaposed, Cohen and Jan in their visceral responses and partisan stances resemble one another more than either would care to admit.

Having read through and reflected on these essays, I would like to elaborate on three points raised in my mind in connection with the arguments and counterarguments presented. They are arranged under the following headings: The Dangers of Ahistoricism; Planning for an Islamic "Reformation": Foolhardy or Intrepid?; and The Historical Trajectory of Moderation.

THE DANGERS OF AHISTORICISM

Cohen's responses are replete with ahistorical generalizations about monolithic Muslims and Muslim societies. Thus he assumes that discriminatory practices against women that now exist in some Muslim countries have been a persistent feature of all Muslim societies at all times. Cohen clearly needs to get a basic education, particularly on the early Islamic period, when Muslim women were more visible in the public sphere, took part in humanitarian, social, and political activities with men, and were prominent in religious education.[1] They enjoyed exclusive rights to their property even after marriage (rights that Western women received only in the nineteenth century) and had considerable freedom in contracting marriages and initiating divorce in certain circumstances. A considerable number of Muslim-majority societies today do not adhere to the gender egalitarianism of the early period, which is a sad commentary on the attrition of Islamic values in such societies and the resurgence of certain cultural practices that clearly violate Qur'anic norms of gender justice.

One particularly telling example is the case of medieval male Muslim exegetes who, starting roughly in the tenth century of the Common Era, began to show a preference for the biblical creation account over the Qur'anic one to justify discriminatory treatment of women. The Qur'an, after all, never singles out Eve for blame in succumbing to Satan's blandishments in Paradise (Qur'an 2:30–39, 7:11–27) and in one account points only to Adam's culpability in the affair (Qur'an 20:115–24). Late medieval exegetes, however, increasingly imported the Genesis story into their commentaries, which disproportionately blames Eve for the Fall and consigns her and her female progeny to a miserable, painful existence on earth in expiation for her "original" sin.[2] Late medieval Islamic societies had grown quite patriarchal and hierarchical under Persian and Hellenist influences in particular, and the biblical Creation story fit the sensibilities of the later medieval period far better than the Qur'anic woman-friendly accounts of the Creation did.

Ijtihad, contrary to Cohen's assumption, has been a hallmark of Sunni as well as of Shia legislative activity up to the present day. The old bromide that "the gate of ijtihad was closed in the tenth century" became a staple of Orientalist discourse concerned with documenting the "fossilization" of

Islamic thought. Incredibly, a significant number of Muslims have internalized this Orientalist discourse about themselves and have deemed this bromide credible. The brilliant legal historian Wael Hallaq of McGill University effectively debunked this myth in an influential article two decades ago.[3] The serious student of Islam no longer subscribes to this view. Thus ijtihad has always been available to Muslims of all stripes, even though the pace of interpretive activity lessened over time as a substantial corpus of positive laws emerged in the medieval period. As most of the commentators have rightly suggested, drastically changed circumstances in the modern period require a large-scale revisitation of the legal corpus and the mining of the variegated Islamic intellectual heritage in order to craft appropriate hermeneutic strategies suited to our times. Several decades from now, we will probably be proclaiming with hindsight that the *Kulturkampf* now underway between politically radicalized Muslims and their moderate and liberal co-religionists was a blessing in disguise, forcing the latter to face the task of responsibly reclaiming their religio-intellectual tradition from the extremists.

Both Cohen's and Jan's belief in the existence of an "Islamic State" in the early Islamic period is woefully ahistorical. This term cannot be found in any source before the modern period. The Arabic word *dawlah* used in the modern period for the nation-state referred to a "dynasty" in the premodern period. As Cohen suggests, in his vision of a reified Islamic state, Jan may indeed be calling for "an Islamist dictatorship"; but for Cohen to assume a congruence between this Islamist paradigm of governance and actual examples taken from history once again displays his alarming ignorance of basic details of Islamic history and civilization. It is alarming particularly because this kind of crude and uninformed perspective continues to nurture the "clash of civilizations" paradigm and feeds the intellectually and morally impoverished discourse concerning "unregenerate" Muslims, similar to the anti-Semitic discourse of an earlier era. History rather informs us that government during the time of the Prophet Muhammad and his four Rightly Guided Caliphs was a loose, informal system in which rank-and-file men and women had a say and a part to play, particularly in choosing their leaders. Women played distinctive roles in politics, education, and humanitarian work, and special solicitude was shown for religious minorities who wished to remain part of the Muslim polity without converting. The famous Charter of Medina drawn up by the Prophet accorded recognition to the Jews as part of the ummah (the Muslim community). Under the premodern welfare system set up by the Prophet's immediate successors, particularly under the second caliph, Umar, Jews and Christians who were economically disadvantaged were entitled to a part of the state revenues.

I am not sure which religion Cohen has in mind when he talks about a "priest-class" in the context of Islamic history. The ulama (the religious scholars of Islam) did not and do not constitute an ordained, sacerdotal class; any adult Muslim, male or female, with the requisite learning may qualify as a scholar. Historically, the ulama have played oppositional roles vis-à-vis the government and often served as mediators between the public and its rulers. I am afraid Cohen has been duped by extremist Islamist rhetoric when he imagines any form of Islamic government to be ipso facto totalitarian, sexist, and intolerant. In the notes at the end of this chapter I recommend for his edification a basic bibliography of works that will help dispel (one hopes) many of his appalling misconceptions.[4]

Calling baldly for the resurrection of the khilafah, as Jan does, however, is simply sloganeering. Calling for the revival of the principles of social justice, tolerance, and ethical behavior that did characterize the time of the Prophet (peace be upon him) and his four righteous successors will and must resonate with most Muslims. Who in the Islamic world today would not echo Jan's touching plea that it be "devoid of palaces, empires, and the monopolization of wealth"?

PLANNING FOR AN ISLAMIC "REFORMATION": FOOLHARDY OR INTREPID?

John Esposito very astutely asks: "Will the process of renewal be one of restoration or reformation (not necessarily the Reformation)?" The term "reformation," for better or for worse, evokes the memory of the European Reformation of the sixteenth century. The term is used positively (mainly by Protestants) in the contemporary West to refer to a much-needed step in the history of Western European Christianity to cleanse it of the detritus of undesirable accretions and innovations that had crept in over centuries. What these very same people conveniently forget is that the Reformation launched a series of brutal wars fanned by religious fanaticism that left hundreds of thousands of people dead. Certainly no one in his or her right mind would wish this on anyone else!

An analogous cleansing process is, however, sorely needed in the Islamic world. I think that the terms "restoration" and "reclamation" are much better suited to this project within Islam, since most modernist and reformist Muslims who would be spearheading such a project wish to "restore" core principles of tolerance and gender equity and "reclaim" the original broad range of meanings of concepts like jihad. Reform will ensue on a much surer footing only when such a project of restoration and reclamation has taken place. Scholars and other molders of public opinion have to show convincingly that principles such as tolerance and gender equity are indeed grounded in religious texts and that the gestalt of the early Muslim community shaped by these core principles can be plausibly retrieved from a close study of early sources. Modernist and reformist Muslims maintain that modern notions of tolerance, respect for diversity, accountable government, and gender parity are already reflected in the Qur'an and in the early praxis of the Muslim community. These notions need to be retrieved and restored as central concepts within Islamic societies today and their ambit expanded through the principled use of ijtihad to become congruent with contemporary notions of human rights and gender equality, for example. Such research is already underway and will sooner or later bring about convincing changes in people's opinion, if and when they are given a fair and extended hearing.

The Historical Trajectory of Moderation

"Moderation" may be considered a fairly weathered term in Islamic thought when one bears in mind that the Qur'an describes Muslims as constituting an *ummah wasat*, a "middle" or "moderate" nation (Qur'an 2:143). Such moderation came to be defined in opposition to *ghuluw*, meaning "exaggeration" (in the sense of falling away from the mean) and "extremism." It is worth pointing out that righteous Jews and Christians also constitute a "balanced (and hence moderate) community," in Arabic *ummah muqtasidah* (Qur'an 5:66). Moderation is thus an attribute of all righteous people regardless of their confessional affiliation, according to the Qur'an, and not only of Muslims by virtue of being Muslim, as Jan is inclined to state. Islamic ethical literature counsels moderation in various aspects of life, including religious observances and abstention from licit pleasures of life. In terms of practicing the faith, an average moderate Muslim in the premodern period was in effect someone who would more or less resemble an average moderate Muslim now. Moderate Muslims practiced their faith more by living it as a private relationship with the Almighty and by adhering to a set of ethical values in relation to their fellow human beings than by sloganeering about political ideology and wearing it as a badge on their sleeve. From this perspective, I agree with John Esposito that the term "moderate Muslim" broadly encompasses traditionalists and nonviolent Islamists in addition to liberal and modernist Muslims.

The term "moderate Muslim" in public American discourse, however, has acquired a bad odor to a certain extent, because it has now become a greatly politicized label in the aftermath of September 11. Aggravating this situation, the term is often conferred as a trophy by career Islamophobes (like Daniel Pipes) on individuals from putative Muslim backgrounds, whose rhetoric and posturing often betray them as fringe Muslim-bashers (Stephen Schwartz is a notable example) once they hit the lucrative neo-con-funded lecture circuit.

Dare we define who a "moderate Muslim" is/should be today? The older definition intimated above still holds true—Islam as a faith and a belief system is of greater primacy for the moderate Muslim than for the immoderate one. Moderate Muslims take pride, for example, that Islamic societies on the whole were kinder to religious minorities than others; that Islam liberated women from the tyranny of fathers and husbands by giving them a say in their marriage, allowing them to hold onto their personal wealth even after marriage, and mandating religious education for all irrespective of gender; that Islam emphasizes spiritual cleansing as a component of jihad, which can also be invoked in military self-defense in dire circumstances; and that the Qur'an instituted *shura*, "mutual consultation," in all aspects of life, particularly the political and administrative. Immoderate, right-wing Muslims—like immoderate right-wing Jews or Christians, for example—tend to take refuge in triumphalism and in a teleological view of history that promises them ultimate victory over all others. Thus immoderate Muslims emphasize the early Muslim conquests of the Levant and Persia, for example, as mandating a continuing quest for world dominion today; stress the military aspect of jihad and discount the spiritual; support the subservience of women to men in highly patriarchal societies; and endorse the socially inferior status of non-Muslim citizens in a reified Islamic state, whose existence is believed to be decreed by scripture itself. "Islam is the solution" is frequently their shibboleth, encapsulating their worldview that religious texts provide ready-made answers in practically all situations to life's complexities and conundrums and that Muslims have nothing to learn from other religions, peoples, and cultures.

A Return to Authenticity or Recourse to Heresy?

A critical mass of Muslims will have to be theologically and intellectually convinced today that the moderate position as identified above remains the historically continuous and authentic one. True, the majority of Muslims are not extremist or militant in their behavior or rhetoric; but many do hold immoderate views regarding women and religious minorities in particular. Retrenchment in the face of a much more economically and militarily powerful West has prompted defensive reactions on the part of Muslims in the heartlands of Islam and a pronounced reluctance to admit that their societies have real problems that are *not* due to the incompetence of U.S. State Department officials or to Israeli malfeasance. It is heartening that a Yemeni judge, Hamoud al-Hitar, has convinced (and continues to convince) scores of Islamist militants today that the Qur'an condemns their violent tactics and has successfully prevailed upon them to renounce their brutal ways and to become rehabilitated in society.[5] Other Muslim scholars in the Islamic world and in the diaspora continue to produce works of scholarship that challenge and undermine extremist and illiberal understandings of religious texts and the law.[6] "The scholars are the heirs of the prophets," and "the ink of the scholar is more precious than the blood of the martyr." These words of the Prophet remind us that knowledge and scholarship have always been paramount in the religious and social fabric of Islamic societies through time, especially in effecting change and renewal. And they still remain the key to a changed and renewed future for Muslims today.

NOTES

1. See, for example, Leila Ahmed, *Women and Gender in Islam* (New Haven: Yale University Press, 1992), 41–78; and my "Reconstituting Women's Lives: Gender and the Poetics of Narrative in Medieval Biographical Works," *Muslim World* 92 (2002): 461–80.

2. See, for example, Barbara Freyer Stowasser, *Women in the Qur'an, Traditions, and Interpretation* (Oxford: Oxford University Press, 1994), "The Chapter of Eve," 25–38.

3. Wael Hallaq, "Was the Gate of *Ijtihad* Closed?" *International Journal of Middle East Studies* 18 (1986): 427–54.

4. I particularly recommend Abdulaziz Sachedina's *The Islamic Roots of Democratic Pluralism* (Oxford: Oxford University Press, 1991); Khaled Abou El Fadl, *The Place of Tolerance in Islam* (Boston: Beacon Press, 2002); and my "Islamic State: Genealogy, Facts, and Myths," *Journal of Church and State* (Winter 2006, forthcoming).

5. See the article by James Brandon, "Koranic Duels Ease Terror," *Christian Science Monitor*, February 4, 2005.

6. Some of their names occur throughout this volume.

CONTRIBUTORS

ARIEL COHEN has been a senior research fellow at the Heritage Foundation since 1992. He is the author of *Russian Imperialism* (Westport, CN: Praeger, 1998) and co-author and editor of *Eurasia in Balance* (Burlington, VT: Ashgate Publishing, 2005).

JOHN L. ESPOSITO is a university professor and the founding director of the Center for Muslim-Christian Understanding at Georgetown University. He is the author of over thirty books on Islam, including the *Unholy War: Terror in the Name of Islam* (Oxford: Oxford University Press, 2002), *What Everyone Needs to Know about Islam* (Oxford: Oxford University Press, 2002), and *Islam: The Straight Path*, 3rd rev. ed. (Oxford: Oxford University Press, 2004).

GRAHAM E. FULLER is a former vice-chair of the National Intelligence Council at the Central Intelligence Agency. He has served as a U.S. Foreign Service Officer in multiple countries of the Middle East for nearly two decades and worked at the RAND Corporation as a senior political scientist on Middle Eastern issues for twelve years. He has written widely on many aspects of Middle Eastern politics. His latest book is The Future of Political Islam (New York: Palgrave Macmillan, 2004).

ABID ULLAH JAN is associated with the Independent Center for Strategic Studies and Analyses, a Canadian think-tank. He is a frequent commentator on Islam and global politics, and his columns are published widely by Muslim media. He is the author of several books, including *A War on Islam?* (Ottawa, Canada: Pragmatic Publishers, 2001) and *The End of Democracy* (Ottawa, Canada: Pragmatic Publishers, 2004).

M. A. MUQTEDAR KHAN is an associate professor in the Department of Political Science and International Relations and director of Islamic Studies at the University of Delaware and a nonresident fellow at the Brookings Institution. He is also associated with the Institute for Social Policy and Understanding. He is the author of *American Muslims: Bridging Faith and Freedom* (Beltsville, MD: Amana, 2002) and *Jihad for Jerusalem: Identity and Strategy in International Relations* (Westport, CN: Praeger, 2004). He is also the editor of *Islamic Democratic Discourse* (Lanham, MD: Lexington Press, 2006).

COMMENTATORS

FEISAL ABDUL RAUF is the imam of Masjid al-Farah in New York City and founder of the American Sufi Muslim Association (ASMA) Society. He is the author of *What's Right with Islam: A New Vision for Muslims and the West* (San Francisco: HarperSanFrancisco, 2004) and *Islam: A Sacred Law—What Every Muslim Should Know about the Shariah* (n.p.: Threshold Books, 1999).

ALI A. MAZRUI is Albert Schweitzer Professor in the Humanities and director of the Institute of Global Cultural Studies at Binghamton University, State University of New York. He is the author of over twenty books, including *The Power of Babel: Language and Governance in the African Experience* (Chicago: University of Chicago Press, 1998) and *Cultural Forces in World Politics* (London: James Currey; and Portsmouth, NH: Heinemann, 1990).

LOUAY SAFI is the executive director of the Islamic Society of North America (ISNA) Leadership Development Center (ILDC), Plainfield, Indiana. He is the author of eight books, including *Tensions and Transitions in the Muslim World* (Lanham, MD: University Press of America, 2003) and *Peace and the Limits of War* (Herndon, VA: International Institute of Islamic Thought, 2001).

MAHMOOD MAMDANI is the Herbert Lehman Professor of Government in the Department of Anthropology at Columbia University. He is also the director of the Institute of African Studies at the School of International and Public Affairs (SIPA). He is the author of the award-winning book *Citizen and Subject: Contemporary Africa and the Legacy of Late Colonial-*

ism (Princeton: Princeton University Press, 1996). His latest book is *Good Muslim, Bad Muslim: America, the Cold War, and the Roots of Terror* (New York: Pantheon, 2004).

M. HAKAN YAVUZ is an associate professor in the Department of Political Science at the University of Utah. He is the author of *Islamic Political Identity in Turkey* (Oxford: Oxford University Press, 2003) and co-editor with John Esposito of *Turkish Islam and the Secular State: The Gülen Movement* (Syracuse: Syracuse University Press, 2003).

TAHA JABIR AL-ALWANI is the president of the Graduate School of Islamic and Social Sciences and holds the Imam al-Shafi'i Chair in Islamic Law. He is the author of *Al Ijtihad wa al Taqlid fi al Islam* (Legal Reasoning and Imitation in Islam) and *Adab al Ikhtilaf fi al Islam* (The Ethics of Disagreement in Islam).

KAMRAN A. BOKHARI is director of analysis, Middle East and South Asia, at the private U.S. intelligence firm Strategic Forecasting, Inc., and a doctoral student in the Department of Political Science at Howard University, Washington, D.C.

FARID SENZAI is a fellow and director of research at the Institute for Social Policy and Understanding and is completing his Ph.D. in the Department of Political Science at Oxford University, U.K.

ASMA AFSARUDDIN is the author of *Excellence and Precedence: Medieval Islamic Discourse on Legitimate Leadership* (Leiden: E. J. Brill, 2002) and the editor of *Hermeneutics and Honor: Negotiation of Female "Public" Space in Islamicate Societies* (Cambridge, MA: Harvard University, 1999). She is an associate professor of Arabic and Islamic studies at the University of Notre Dame.

INDEX